D1058447

ENDORSEMENTS

Rarely does God combine prophetic gifts with pastoral gifts. Many prophets are so high upon the wall they lose contact with the sheep they are guarding. Many pastors are so close to the ground that they, like the sheep, are grazing in green pastures oblivious to the shifting seasons through which the sheep travel. It is through the man, the ministry, and the message of Larry Titus that a unique spiritual blend of a prophet's voice, a father's love, and a shepherd's heart that a sanctified relationship of spiritual parenting evolves. Like Father Abraham, he has many sons and daughters, but most of all he is an instrument, an inspiration, and an encouragement to a shifting generation with the revelation that God desires to turn the heart of the fathers to their children and the heart of the children to their fathers. If you need a model of manhood fused with fatherhood—cautiously read this book!

> — Bishop Kenneth C. Ulmer, D.Min., Ph.D.
> Senior Pastor of Faithful Central Bible Church

The example and imprint of the life and voice of Larry Titus is deeply acknowledged by two of my close friends and colleagues in ministry, Pastors Jimmy Evans and Tom Lane. When they were young men, it was Larry who released the "teleios" in them. His example and articulation takes men to their full potential—beyond what they can see for themselves. Read *The Teleios Man* and allow Larry's input to imprint you as he has done for multitudes.

> —Robert Morris
> Senior Pastor, Gateway Church
> Best-Selling Author, *The Blessed Life*

I highly recommend this book and the ministry of Larry Titus to you. Larry has deeply impacted my life and the lives of many other men I know. He lives what he teaches and is an example for all men who want to live for Christ.

—Jimmy Evans
Founder and President, MarriageToday
Senior Elder, Trinity Fellowship Church, Amarillo, Texas
Author, *Marriage on the Rock*

In *The Teleios Man*, Larry Titus shows the heart of a spiritual father: to show a man his true identity as a son. He sees with spiritual eyes the intrinsic worth and potential hidden in a man, calls him forth into his destiny by encouraging words and actions, affirms his giftings as they emerge, and prophetically seals the calling of God by blessing him. This restoration of the father-son relationship is the great need and the ultimate destiny of our generation.

—Conard F. Failinger, MD
Morgantown, West Virginia

the TELEIOS MAN

the TELEIOS MAN

Your *ultimate* Identity

LARRY TITUS

DEVELOPMENT SERVICES, INC

Oviedo, Florida

The Teleios Man—Your Ultimate Identity
by Larry Titus

Published by HigherLife Development Services, Inc.
400 Fontana Circle
Building 1—Suite 105
Oviedo, Florida 32765
(407) 563-4806
www.ahigherlife.com

This book or parts thereof may not be reproduced in any form, stored in a retrieval system, or transmitted in any form by any means—electronic, mechanical, photocopy, recording, or otherwise—without prior written permission of the publisher, except as provided by United States of America copyright law.

Unless otherwise noted, Scripture quotations are from *The Holy Bible: NEW INTERNATIONAL VERSION*®. Copyright © 1973, 1978, 1984 by Biblica, Inc. All rights reserved worldwide. Used by permission.

Scripture quotations noted KJV are from *The Holy Bible: King James Version*. Cambridge, 1769. Used by permission. All rights reserved.

Scripture quotations noted NKJV are from the *New King James Version*. Copyright © 1982 Thomas Nelson Inc. Used by permission. All rights reserved.

Scripture quotations noted *The Message* are from *The Message*. Copyright © 1993, 1994, 1996, 2000, 2001, 2002. Used by permission of NavPress Publishing Group.

Scripture quotations noted NASB are from the *New American Standard Bible*®. Copyright © 1960, 1962, 1963, 1968, 1971, 1972, 1973, 1975, 1977, 1995 by the Lockman Foundation. Used by permission.

Scripture quotations noted NLT are from the *Holy Bible, New Living Translation*. Copyright © 1996 and 2004. Used by permission of Tyndale House Publishers, Wheaton, Illinois 60189. All rights reserved.

Copyright © 2010 by Larry Titus
All rights reserved

ISBN 13: 978-1-935245-29-2
ISBN 10: 1-935245-29-5

Cover Design: r2cdesign—Rachel Lopez
Second Edition
12 13 14 15 – 9 8 7 6 5 4 3 2
Printed in the United States of America

Dedication

Devi

My wife

My love

My strength

My support

My encourager

My friend

My inspiration

My balance

Generations of Righteousness

In addition to my beautiful wife, Devi, I want to dedicate this book to my awesome children, Trina and Aaron. They are the joy of my life. Their character and life choices have fulfilled my dreams as a father. What on earth can surpass the joy of seeing your children serving and loving God fervently; only one thing, seeing your grandchildren replicating their examples. So to my children's children, Brooke, Brandon, Brittany, Bryson, Melody and Michaela, I also dedicate this book. You have made my life complete. Well, not quite, there are the great grandchildren, Sophia, Isabella, Brielle, Levi, Landon, Anderson. So I bless and dedicate this book to them as well. Then there's...

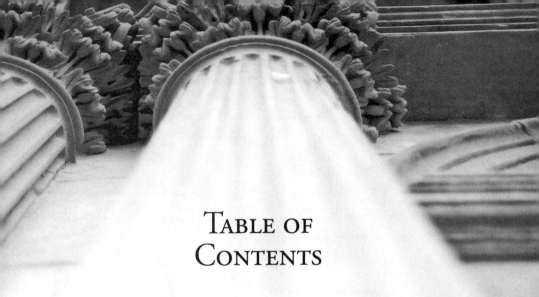

TABLE OF CONTENTS

FOREWORD

I T'S BEEN TWENTY YEARS since I heard one of my favorite quotes. Its appeal to me is the way it cuts to the core—being more than just clever, it's *Christ-like:*

"The main thing is to keep the main thing the main thing!"

I hope it doesn't offend anyone that it isn't a quote from the Bible, especially since I said I see it as very much "like" Jesus. But I'll stand by it, because what Jesus modeled in the way he spent his time indicates "the main thing" as he saw it. Jesus's ministry spent more time on "discipling men" than anything else.

That's what this book is about—discipleship. It's about *shaping, growing, mentoring, teaching, nurturing guys* in ways that they become *very real* though <u>not</u> "very religious." It's about precisely the same thing Jesus did in laying the groundwork for establishing his church.

1. Yes, he died to provide salvation for humankind and birthed the possibility for his church.
2. Yes, he rose from the dead, and in verifying his cross did achieve #1; he gave the church a life-giving message.
3. Yes, he sent his Spirit, pouring out "power from on high" to enable the church—his people—to effectively "go into all the world" with his works as well as his Word (Luke 24:49, Mark 16:15).

But Jesus focused on discipling men. There's no reason to apologize for that as though he was or is indifferent to women. His ministry not only elevated the place of women in his day, but also timelessly opened doors of purpose and ministry for women, overthrowing ancient traditions of male chauvinism. But nonetheless, his first priority was discipling men. He invested an incredible amount of time enabling a group of men to find their way past the habits, syndromes, preoccupations, and patterns that tend to trap guys.

This is the pattern the living church has employed from that day to this, and where leaders "get" this, they always welcome resources that help cultivate effective ministry to men. That's why I'm so happy to introduce this book by Larry Titus.

Larry has a plan for "springing the traps," and I've seen the evidence of what happens when men open to the kind of "male liberation" his resources provide. Whether as a writer, as a pastor, as a teacher, as a one-to-one mentor, as a small-group or large-crowd speaker, as a counselor, or as an apostolic missionary to nations, Larry effectively communicates with and helps men become what real discipleship in Christ can make them.

This handbook may be his best condensation of those principles—a dynamic handbook you can use, sir—as a leader with others, as a buddy teaming with another to move forward in Christ together, or simply as a discipling plan to get started on your own.

So make "the main thing the main thing." Get into discipling men—beginning with the man God can bring you to be yourself. This book will help you use The Book to get there: It's "the right stuff."

The Teleios Man is for God and for guys, because when husbands grow, wives win; and as men grow, women are freed.

—Jack Hayford
Chancellor, The King's University and Seminary
Founding Pastor, The Church On the Way

PREFACE

WHEN I WAS EIGHTEEN years old, I was touched by a profound event that shaped the rest of my life. I was in only the second semester of my freshman year of Bible College, training for ministry and already out of money. My elderly dad was no longer able to assist in paying for my education. He'd suffered a stroke and couldn't work. My mom was a traveling full-time evangelist and was barely making ends meet. I was working, but it wasn't enough. I passionately loved learning, but my dreams of a college education seemed to be slipping away. I couldn't do anything about it. That's when it happened. A man stepped into my life and changed the course of my future.

Suddenly, the threatening notices I'd been getting from the college accounting office stopped. They were replaced by statements reflecting inexplicable payments on my college account balance.

After a little investigating and persuasive coaxing, I discovered the name of my benefactor. He was my Greek-Hebrew professor. I went to him immediately.

"Dr. Rider, you shouldn't be paying on my account. You don't make enough money to do that!"

"On the contrary," he responded, "we *do* need to pay on your account. You see, when my wife and I were first married, we decided that rather than investing in stocks and bonds we would invest in people. We're not just paying on your bill, Larry; we're investing in your future. That way, wherever you go, and whomever you reach for Jesus, part of the dividend will return to us."

Since that day, I have also invested in people. People of all sizes, shapes, walks of life, economic status, races, or religious backgrounds have been part of my investment portfolio. I want to see people, especially men, change and become all that God intended them to be—*Teleios* Men. My goal is to intentionally influence every man I see for Christ.

Yes, during my fifty years of ministry, and with thirty-four of those years as a Senior Pastor, I have invested in men. I call them. I spend time with them. I take men on ministry trips, pray with them, e-mail them, and disciple them. I've helped pay for their educations, mission trips, seminary degrees, and clothes. I've sent birthday cards, given money to their children, chipped in on special projects, helped them start their own businesses, married them, helped them pay for their honeymoons, dedicated their babies, and helped load their moving vans. I've walked with them through trials and preached at funerals when their loved ones passed away.

I have invested in men on every continent—thousands of them. At all times and in all places, I have with great determination invested in men. I fervently believe a great monument has been built as a memorial to the godly professor who invested in me. His dividends have accrued and, through Christ, he's realized immense returns.

The first time I preached in India, a crowd of 35,000 had already gathered. I was waiting to meet my interpreter before walking out onto the stage. "Do you remember me?" he said. "My name is K.C. John. I came to the United States planning to attend Bible College, but didn't have the funds. Someone brought me to your church, and you took up an offering for me so I could enroll." I was stunned! Amazing! The man who was to be my first interpreter in India was the same young man we'd invested in years earlier by paying for his tuition. My professor's investment was continuing to grow!

The years left in my own life are fewer and fewer, and I deeply pray for a way to expand my circle of teaching and coaching, which is my own investment. This book was birthed by the desperate yearning of my heart to train and coach the innumerable men yet to have anyone invest in their lives. I say to these men that although it is unlikely I will ever meet you, I want to instill in you the essential principles I have gleaned and taught over these past five decades. Then you can pass them on to others! I would love to be your spiritual dad if I could, but I can't. So I'm passing on to you the treasures of my heart in hopes that you will pass them on to other men I cannot possibly reach.

The ultimate man, biblically, is the Teleios Man. Teleios, pronounced *TEL*-ee-ahss from the Greek word meaning, "to complete, to finish, to perfect—nothing else needed," is God's will for you. When Jesus said on the cross, "It is finished," the Greek uses *teleios* as Jesus's "finished."

I want you to be that Teleios Man—the finished, completed man—who has learned and modeled truths that ensure balance and maturity. I want to teach you things that will be part of your future and the generations which follow you. I'm passing on to you my heart's desire to invest in people and glorify Christ.

Men, this is my goal for you. I want you to find that place of completion in Christ. You *can* enter into his new identity for you.

In Jesus's love and kingdom,

— Larry Titus

ACKNOWLEDGEMENTS

I WANT TO ACKNOWLEDGE MY gratitude for several people who have made this book possible. First and foremost is my wife, Devi. Her wisdom and insight are woven through every page of this book. It's impossible for me to speak or write without feeling the grace of her influence. Devi consistently gives me spiritual, emotional, and intellectual gifts from her rich stores of experience. Using a loving sensitivity and knowledge, she ceaselessly encourages and affirms me. This book could never have been written without her sagacity and inspiration.

You will read Larry Lee's story in Chapter 4, "Healing the Father Wound." Larry's contribution here has been immense. His biblical insights, spirituality, and writing skills helped this book grow from concept to completion. Larry's intellectual scope and spiritual integrity guided my writing in many pages of this book. His help was simply indispensable.

Editing expertise and constructive advice was also given by Cristina Papson. Cristina is a former Deputy Attorney General for the State of Pennsylvania. Cristina's husband, Michael Papson, is a top financial advisor for a major corporation. He added valuable tips on investing included in Chapter 10, "O Debt, Where Is Your Sting?" Michael and Cristina have been our friends for years. They provided assistance with this book and have shared our vision to reach the world with the gospel. We're joined together at the heart and have spent many hours of fun and fruitful fellowship together.

Michael Weiher and his wife, Marilyn, did final editorial work and judged the jots and tittles of my work. Michael is a music teacher and choir director. He's also gifted in the written word. Michael made significant contributions to Chapter 11, "We Are Each One of a Kind, Thank God." Over the past decade, Michael and Marilyn have been close faithful friends and stuck to me like Band-Aids.

Jeff Hamilton, a longtime friend and member of our first ministry in Washington, took my finished manuscript and added invaluable insights, wisdom, and improved text in virtually every chapter. Jeff knows me so well, having lived for a short season in our home during his early college years. He has an ability to turn mediocre material into outstanding copy and content. Thank you for coming along at the right time, Jeff, not only for this book but also for me.

Fifty years of ministry and thousands of men have contributed to this book. I've personally met and spoken with these men at conferences, churches, prisons, retreats, and private counseling sessions. We've exchanged even more thousands of phone calls, letters, and emails. Of course, these lives have affected and deeply transformed my own life. The names of only a few of these men appear in the pages of this book, yet *all* the names and lives have been branded on my memory and heart. Without exception, each one has made me a better man.

There is One alone in heaven and on earth truly worthy of praise. A choir in heaven sings, "Worthy is the Lamb who was slain, to receive power and wealth and wisdom and strength and honor and glory and praise" (Rev. 5:12). Yet the heavenly singing fails to capture the gratefulness of a fallen race redeemed by grace alone. My paltry efforts as one humble writer depend on breath given by Christ's sustaining love. Without Jesus Christ, there is no book, no marriage, and no eternal forgiveness. There are no friends, ministry, reality, love, or meaning. Only God's perfect Teleios Man, Jesus Christ, shows us the way to true completeness. To Jesus alone I give all praise, thanksgiving, and gratitude. I will see him face to face one day, and I will be eternally grateful knowing that this book is his—*all for him and all about him.*

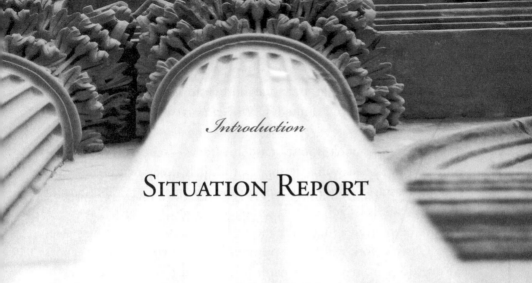

SITUATION REPORT

M OST MEN IN AMERICA and the rest of the world are in a horrible state. They have lost their way. Their self-images are blurry and confused. We are now entering into the third generation of men who have grown up in dysfunctional families and have no clue what they are to do and be in life. Men are desperately in need of someone who will believe in them, encourage them, disciple them, and empower them. These men are also in need of specific practical guidance in what it means to be godly, mature, and balanced husbands. They need to know how to be fathers and leaders.

Christ's work in the past is our resource in the here and now. We reach back to the cross for our salvation. We reach back to the atonement in the perfect sacrifice of Christ for our righteousness. We reach back to the stripes on Jesus's back for our healing. We reach back to Christ's victory in the wilderness for our victory over temptation. Finally, we reach back to the foundation of the earth where God designed us, before time began, to find our identity and future purpose in life.

You've been given a huge gift, and you're about to hear just how staggering Christ's work will be in your life.

Men who sincerely want to see their lives changed generally start from the failures of the past and work forward. This simply won't work. It's like telling a child all his life what a failure he is, then expecting him to have a mind-set of success. *This book is about starting at the end and working backward.* You're already perfect in Christ.

It's not something you do, but something Jesus has already finished for you. The Father sees you through Christ! Now it's up to you to work on the details.

The goal of this book is to start as Christ does—start with the present reality and work backwards. Rather than futilely dredging up your past, I'm going to start with the finished work of Christ and show you how to progress forwards by going *backwards to the life of Christ.*

You've been given a huge gift, and you're about to hear just how staggering Christ's work will be in your life. I can tell you to expect echoes and questions from your old nature that could diminish the work of Jesus. They'll sound something like the following:

- ❑ "What about my sins?"
  - ✓ *They've already been forgiven!*

- ❑ "What about my sinful nature?"
  - ✓ *You have a new nature where sin is not natural!*

- ❑ "What about the memory of my sins?
  - ✓ *Your sins have been covered by the blood of Christ and thrown into the sea of forgetfulness!*

- ❑ "What about my old man?"
  - ✓ *He's dead and doesn't exist any longer!*

- ❑ "And those stubborn habit patterns and temptations, what about them?"
  - ✓ *Christ already triumphed over every form of temptation without sinning, and you became the righteousness of God in Christ. You are sharing in his victory.*

- ❑ "How will other people see me?"
  - ✓ *Probably as you were, but it doesn't matter, as long as you see yourself as Christ sees you.*

❑   "How then can I be perfect?"
    ✓   *In Christ you already are. You are a Teleios Man!*

So, stay with me, and let's get back to the lesson plan. In Christ, the past is gone. At the moment you received Jesus as your Lord and Savior, all his righteousness and perfection became yours. Now, change your behavior to comport with your new status! This book is designed to help you do that. I'm coaching you, and I've seen these principles work consistently and successfully! It's *not* a matter of you attaining perfection; you are perfect *already* through Christ. It simply means that you conform to your new image—your new man.

Key concepts in the strategy to help each of us conform to Christ in the new man:

*   The Teleios Man knows that his victory comes from letting Christ live through him.

*   The Teleios Man doesn't use self-defeating phrases like "Well, I'm not perfect." He chooses to live in Christ's perfection and speak in affirming language.

*   The Teleios Man isn't sinless in his behavior but strives to sin less.

*   The Teleios Man chooses to put Christ, his wife, and family above all other interests.

*   The Teleios Man brings his body, soul, mind, and spirit into subjection to Christ.

*   The Teleios Man makes Christ his goal in all things and seeks to replicate the life of Jesus and live in his perfection.

Your whole life should conform to one thing. *God has already created you perfect in Christ!* Your job is to start looking like who you *are* rather than who you *were*.

Paul states in 2 Corinthians 5:21: "He made him who knew no sin to be sin on our behalf, so that we might become the righteousness of God in him" (NASB). Is that mind-boggling, or what? When we receive Christ, we trade Him all our sin and unrighteousness, for His perfection and righteousness.

For additional scriptures that relate to your new position in Christ, I recommend the reading and memorization of the following verses:

- Colossians 3:1-3—Since, then, you have been raised with Christ, set your hearts on things above, where Christ is seated at the right hand of God. Set your minds on things above, not on earthly things. For you died and your life is now hidden with Christ in God.

- 2 Corinthians 5:17—Therefore, if anyone is in Christ, he is a new creation; the old has gone, the new has come!

- Galatians 2:20—I have been crucified with Christ and I no longer live, but Christ lives in me. The life I live in the body, I live by faith in the Son of God, who loved me and gave himself for me.

- James 1:4—But let patience have *its* perfect work, that you may be perfect and complete, lacking nothing. (NKJV)

- Romans 6:4-7—Therefore, we were buried with Him through baptism into death, that just as Christ was raised from the dead by the glory of the Father, even so we also should walk in newness of life. For if we have been united together in the likeness of his death, certainly we also shall be *in the likeness of his resurrection*, knowing this, that our old man was crucified with *Him*, that the body of sin might be done away with, that we should no longer be slaves of sin. For he who has died has been freed from sin. (NKJV)

- Ephesians 4:13—Till we all come in the unity of the faith, and of the knowledge of the Son of God, unto a perfect man, unto the measure of the stature of the fullness of Christ. (KJV)

- Colossians 1:28—Whom we preach, warning every man, and teaching every man in all wisdom; that we may present every man perfect in Christ Jesus. (KJV)

Chapter 1

Your Identity

"I'M AWESOME— YOU'RE INCREDIBLE"

I WAS SPEAKING AT A men's retreat in the Colorado Rockies. Out in the assembly of guys, I noticed a man who seemed beset with a heavy depression. While the other men worshiped, "Craig" mumbled the words and seemed lost in an inner wrestling match, a torment that kept him constantly looking downward and perplexed. My heart went out to him, and I prayed for an opportunity to share and pray together.

We soon met, and I listened as Craig began to tell me about his life. He was two years old when his parents divorced. Through his early years, he was shuttled between his mother, father, and grandmother. When he was 13, his grandmother took him to his dad's house for a visit. He ran inside to greet him, but his father lay there dead on the sofa. A tape recorder with empty reels ran spinning next to the body.

Beside the lifeless body, Craig numbly rethreaded the tape and heard his father say, "Craig, you're the reason I'm killing myself." The tape ended with the sounds of labored breathing, and then there was no sound.

Craig ran out the back door and began living on the streets of Denver. He stole food from drunks and slept in dumpsters. During the nights, he kept his ears keen for the garbage trucks.

One night, while he was sound asleep, Craig didn't hear a front-end loader coming, and it scooped up the dumpster with him inside. His body didn't fall into the compactor, or no one would have seen or heard of Craig again. Instead, he fell onto the windshield of the truck and was taken promptly to the police station.

It was appropriate that Craig should be living in a garbage dumpster because that's how he saw himself—just garbage, a young son who'd caused his father's suicide.

During that retreat in the Rockies, I was able to share with Craig the truth that he wasn't responsible for his dad's death. His dad, I said, had made his own tragic decision to end his life. Then I began to explain to him how special he was and how much God loved him. Though his earthly father had failed him, his Heavenly Father never would. I went on to describe how much God had invested in his life and what an incredible future God had in mind for him.

One thing I can't stand is to see a young man without a father. I'll happily adopt him on the spot. As I put my arms around Craig, I voiced what his real father hadn't been able to say, "I love you, Craig, and I'm proud of you." With those words and that embrace, the pent-up emotions from years of anger, hurt, rejection, and fear began to come up out of deep places in Craig. He sobbed softly, and his heart began to melt. He was being set free.

The next day while I was driving out of the camp, Craig saw me, rolled down his window and, with the biggest smile a man could have, yelled, "I love you!"

My experience with Craig is not unusual. In fact, it's a very common story in the world today. Over the years, I have counseled with hundreds of men whose self-image was virtually destroyed during their painful and abusive youth. These guys grew up wounded, and they limped through life. Even after coming into Christ and receiving the forgiveness of sins and experiencing new birth, they still struggled with how they saw themselves. Even more devastating was how they imagined God must see them. Someone had lied to them, and they internalized the lie and found no healing or balm.

How deep is the "father wound" in these men! I've seen men build huge fortunes and work themselves into a stumbling fatigue as they tried to heal father-wounds. Men build muscular bodies in weight rooms as they hope to defend themselves against more wounding. Men look for solace in serial relationships with women. Other men use intoxicants in hopes of having a fleeting moment or two where their pain is forgotten. In prisons, I've seen the hard, determined faces of inmates suddenly wet with tears as they talk about their father-wounds.

Consistently, I have grieved and wept with men who still bled from tremendous past abuse and rejection from their fathers. Some of these guys didn't even have a father–a "father-wound" that cuts even deeper.

There is an enormously simple but devastatingly cruel equation not solved in the lives of these men. While there are truths of rebirth in Christ in these men, there are also deeply felt beliefs of unworthiness before God. They solve all this by incorrectly believing that God's love is qualified. Their algebra is wrong and they think they are born again, yet they feel unworthy and that God's love for them is somehow qualified. These wounded men expect God to strike them at any moment—like their fathers did. They know that God could capriciously reject them—like their fathers did. Who could freely and exuberantly worship such a God?

You must begin seeing yourself in a new light, and that means seeing yourself in exactly the same way God sees you—incredible!

You Are Incredibly Special to God

Before you can become the Teleios Man (the acclaimed man God has called you to be), your thinking must change. You must begin seeing yourself in a new light, and that means seeing yourself in exactly the same way God sees you—incredible! You must agree with God and know how special you are. He thinks you're *awesome*. This is not religious rhetoric. God thinks so highly of you that he has been investing in you since before your birth. He has plans for your life! In fact, He's been planning your life before time began. Check out some of these themes and verses in the Bible.

- For he chose us in him before the creation of the world… (Eph. 1:4)
- In him we were also chosen, having been predestined according to the plan of him who works out everything in conformity with the purpose of his will. (Eph. 1:11)
- But when God, who set me apart from birth... (Gal. 1:15)
- For we are God's workmanship, created in Christ Jesus to do good works, which God prepared in advance for us to do. (Eph. 2:10)
- For you created my inmost being; you knit me together in my mother's womb. I praise you because I am fearfully and wonderfully made; your works are wonderful, I know that full well…All the days ordained for me were written in your book before one of them came to be. (Ps. 139:13-14,16)
- Before I formed you in the womb I knew you, before you were born I set you apart... (Jer. 1:5)
- For I know the plans I have for you," declares the Lord, "plans to prosper you and not to harm you, plans to give you hope and a future. (Jer. 29:11)
- …being confident of this, that he who began a good work in you will carry it on to completion until the day of Christ Jesus. (Phil. 1:6)

The Scripture teaches that God dwells in eternity rather than the constraints of humanly imagined time. Psalm 90:2: reads, "Before the mountains were born or you brought forth the earth and the world, from everlasting to everlasting you are God." We might say that human time is completely encapsulated or even "swallowed up" in eternity.

Because God is eternal and sovereign, by his foreknowledge he knows all things before they become "history." For example, Acts 2:23 and 4:28 make it clear that Jesus was delivered up for crucifixion by the determined foreknowledge and deliberate hand of God. The Romans and Jews merely carried out this plan. Your salvation, according to John 1:13, didn't occur because you, your relatives, or any other human being determined it. It was God who caused His Spirit to generate life in you by

His sovereign will. As Paul says in Ephesians 1:4, we were chosen in Him before time began.

You Look Just Like Your Father

Have you ever heard someone say, "You look just like your father"? In Genesis 1:27 and 1 Corinthians 11:7, we learn God made us in His image. The Greek word for "image" is *icon*. You are a direct reflection and representation, an icon, of your Creator. You were molded in His image. You have His creative nature inside you. He knit you together in your mother's womb; you are fearfully and wonderfully made (Ps. 139:13-14). Someone said that if God had a refrigerator, He would stick a picture of you on His refrigerator door. I believe that. Since you're made in His image, you are incredibly special to Him. Like any doting parent, God would delight in looking at your photograph on His fridge.

Someone else said, "Jesus had you personally in mind when he hung on the cross." I can't argue with that. I'm certain He did. But His love for each of us goes back even before the cross two thousand years ago. God's love extends all the way back to the foundation of the universe when He purposed you in His mind. You see, according to the scriptures referenced above, you were no accident. Not even in those human situations where a child is conceived by "mistake" were you an accident in God's mind. There are no accidents with God. God planned, designed, and specifically purposed your personal destiny before the creation of the world. He didn't start knitting you in your mother's womb without first lovingly drawing a pattern of you. Now, the Holy Spirit works continually on earth to bring about what the Father ordained before time began.

Everything about your marvelously complex DNA, your purpose, and your destiny was designed by our Creator in eternity long before time began. God wasn't idly working on His creation. You were not clay thrown against a cosmic wall by a bored God. No! You are the direct result of His creative mind, and you are made in His image. Please take a moment to ponder that. It should thrill, excite, and sober you to imagine you come from God's sovereign, predetermined, and loving design.

After each of God's creative days in Genesis, Chapter 1, he responded with the Hebrew word, *tov* meaning "good." God proclaimed that the first through the fifth days were all "tov" or "good." But when he made Adam, God's reaction, as the original Hebrew translation records it, was "Good, Good!" According to the "Larry Titus amplified, expanded, and emphasized translation," after God created you, he said, "Wow! I really did a great job with him! He's Good, Good!" I can see him clapping his hands and beaming with joy at his accomplishment. When God created you, he placed his nature inside you. Inside you is his DNA, his image, his creative abilities, his personality, and his ability to imagine. Yet he made you *unique*. God created you to be special. There is no one else like you in the world. You're an original masterpiece.

People will often take a verbal swipe at those they consider "originals" because of their idiosyncrasies. They sarcastically note, "When he made you, he really broke the mold."

Actually, this is more accurate than they realize. But it's not just a few "unique" people that God created as originals—it's everyone. You are the only one like you in the world, and I can say, "Praise God for that!" without even a hint of sarcasm. I am grateful for your originality, and I praise God for your uniqueness.

Understanding how God sees you and how he values you is key to changing how you see and value yourself. Numbers 13:33 says, "We seemed like grasshoppers in our own eyes and we looked the same to them." These words were spoken fourteen hundred years before Christ by ten of the twelve returning spies as they reported to the nation of Israel their experiences in the land of Canaan. The spies hadn't truly spoken with giants, whose appearance they had just exaggerated. They had no way of really knowing what the giants thought of them. Could this have been a description of how they thought of themselves?

Ten early intelligence experts brought back an inaccurate report. Two million Israelites believed their story and spent the night crying. Why could only two men, Joshua and Caleb (two men out of two million people), see the same giants but return with a hopeful report, "Certainly we can kill those giants." And eventually they did. Out of the entire multitude of that first generation of Israelites, Joshua and Caleb were the only men whom God would eventually allow to cross into the promised land.

Two hundred and fifty years later, a shepherd boy named David, armed with one smooth stone and the name of the Lord, destroyed Goliath, a giant of giants. Apparently, an army isn't required when fighting giants. One person can do it! But that one person won't see himself as a "grasshopper." He'll think of himself as having the heart and skill and the blessing of God for giant killing.

You must change the way you think about yourself. No one else can do this. But I am here to show you how! Whether you become a grasshopper or a giant killer in life depends on how you picture yourself. If your self-image is that of a nondescript failure, an average Joe, a loser—stop!—you have the wrong picture! I emphatically tell you God sees you as a giant killer! You are not a grasshopper, and you're just as likely to slay threatening giants!

Most men simply do not think highly enough of themselves, and if some guys have a healthy self-respect, they might be accused of arrogance. Do you know I've rarely seen a man I consider truly arrogant. And many apparently arrogant men are only putting up defensive walls.

Our Sense of Self-Worth and Value

Perhaps some of us are in the small minority of men born into balanced homes where unqualified love was freely given. A healthy sense of self-worth came naturally in an affirming, empowering environment. Dad and Mom were both available to train and nurture, and the result was an internal sense of security, value, and self-worth.

Many other men grew up in an emotionally-risky environment brought about by an absentee, disconnected, aloof, demanding, dysfunctional, performance-driven, alcoholic, or abusive dad. These sons had to find their own self-worth, and it was inevitably a self-worth based on external factors. If that's you, these factors included your looks, your intellect, your athletic prowess, your muscles, your musical abilities, your skill in attracting girls, your car, your ability to make money, your toughness, or, in some cases, your bad behavior.

After high school or college, still driven by performance, you had to deal with your low self-esteem. You probably traded your younger value system for the validation offered in the workplace. You thought, "After all, if I do well in my occupation, I'll begin feeling good about myself again." And you'll have to admit that all those "feel good" abilities you had in middle school and high school were rapidly evaporating. The muscles start to flatten out, the football and basketball knees give out, the hair thins, the brain cells start to die, your stomach starts to stick out, and the girls vanish.

So as youthful external factors grow less relevant, the work environment provides new ways of measuring yourself. But what happens if things don't pan out in the workforce? What if you lose your job or fall short of a quota? What if others are promoted ahead of you? What do you do if your compensation always falls short of your family's needs?

Eventually, all those external factors that gave you self-worth will disintegrate and disappoint. You'll find only the value God places on you brings real and lasting meaning. It's based on how God sees you. It's based on his unqualified love for you. It's based on your willingness to see yourself as God sees you.

True self-worth doesn't come from anything we accomplish or acquire.

True self-worth doesn't come from anything we accomplish or acquire. It comes only from the value God himself has placed on us *because we are his creation.* Since your true value, self-esteem, and inner sense of worth can only really come from God, then it's time to start viewing yourself in an entirely new light. No longer can you judge yourself by what you do or have. *In God's eyes, you are awesome—not by anything you have done, but only by what he has done.* I continually tell men, "You're awesome, and you can't even help it. God made you that way."

What Happens When You Belittle Yourself?

What happens when you condemn or belittle yourself? Consider that God knew you before time began and made you in his image. What happens when you attack yourself? If you tear yourself down, you are directly challenging God's opinion of you. If God thinks you're spectacular and you think you're inferior, you have no congruency with God. God is always right, and until you see things his way, you will never be at peace.

To think less of yourself than God does results in low self-esteem. If you believe in yourself and see yourself as God does—as totally awesome—that is not arrogance. It's merely agreeing with God. For you to bring glory to God, you must agree with his assessment of you. You must think and say to yourself on a regular basis, "I'm incredible because God made me that way." And if and when someone compliments you for anything, graciously accept the compliment but inwardly say, "That's for you, God, because you made me that way."

As I write this, I fervently hope you can receive my advice as you would from a trusted father or coach. I encourage you to awaken every day and immediately begin praising God. I want you to say, "Thank you, God, for making me an awesome man. That's the way you created me, and I give you all the glory. You made me a jewel. I may be a diamond in the rough, but I am still a jewel of high quality and value. You made me to succeed, not fail. You began grooming me before I was ever born, and you're still working with me for your good. I will continually praise you for that. Thank you for making me in your image. Thank you for putting your creative energy, image, and abilities inside me. Thank you for having a plan for my life even before I was born. And even though I might not know all of it now, someday I will. Until then, I will trust you. I have been fearfully and wonderfully made, just the way you wanted me. Until the day arrives when you have fully revealed your glory in me, I will continue to praise you for making me special. I'm awesome, and I have you to thank for it."

Awesome or Arrogant?

The religious legalists among us may worry that such thinking will result in an arrogant attitude. To keep your awesomeness from becoming arrogance, just remember that everything you are and have comes from God. Without him you can do nothing. I love Pat Robertson's anecdote,

"It would have been very foolish for the donkey that carried Jesus into Jerusalem to assume that the people were applauding it rather than Jesus." Never forget who the donkey is and who the rider is. Again, I really don't think arrogance is a problem for most men. Quite the contrary, most men think they're the donkey.

Men will often say to me, "I'm just not worthy." My response to that is, "Who is?" Revelation 5 says that no one in heaven or on earth is worthy, only Jesus. Worthiness is not the question here! If we are worthy, why do we need grace? No, the point is: you may not be worthy, but you are irreplaceable. God made you exactly the way he wanted you, and he loves you as you are.

Your abilities, talents, personality, looks, and success all come from God. I have him to praise if my life produces anything of value, and only myself to blame if it doesn't because I failed to accept who I am in him. It is by his grace that I am who I am, and without him I can do nothing. I can never forget that. You're either a grasshopper or a giant killer, and how you think of yourself is what determines the outcome. I hope I can meet you one of these days! I love to meet incredible people. You and I both know that you're awesome because God made you that way.

The Others Are Also Incredible

This is so important I'm going to insist you read this sentence twice. *After you understand how important and special you are to God, you must also understand how important his other children are to him.* (Please read that one more time.) It is not enough for you to know that in God you're awesome. You must also see others as God sees them—equally awesome!

Jesus made it clear in Matthew 19:19 that you must love your neighbor as you love yourself. Remember this notion of "self" love may at first blush seem selfish or self-centered. But I believe there is an important truth to be learned in this verse. First, it is clear Jesus is commanding us to love others. That may seem simple enough, but it's been my observation that men tend to see and treat others as they see themselves. If we see ourselves as garbage, we become defensive and angry. Then we treat our brothers and sisters poorly.

If you cannot love yourself, it is impossible to love your wife, your children, or your neighbor without qualification. Unless you can say, "I'm awesome—I'm incredible," and truly believe it, you cannot fully express God's nature. Neither can you fully love others. Jesus told you what to do in Matthew 19:19. You must love your neighbor as you love yourself.

Here's another truism. Some of the most selfish people in the world are those who have very low self-esteem! So if you want to move from a life of selfishness to a life that values others as being more important than you, you must learn to affirm yourself. I'm repeating this because it is a key to my teaching in this book: Self-affirmation is merely praising God for who he made you to be, nothing more and nothing less.

One of the more puzzling and bizarre miracles that Jesus did was to heal a man twice. I doubt that Jesus intended to give this miracle a second go-around, but until I die or Jesus returns (so I can ask him personally) I'm left to ask the question, "What in the world was going on?" The miracle took place in Bethsaida, a fishing village just a stone's throw north of Galilee. Bethsaida was the home town of Philip, Andrew, and Peter.

A blind man was led to Jesus, and his friends asked Jesus to touch him. This puzzling incident is found in Mark 8:22-26. Instead of touching him, Jesus spit into the man's blind eyes then asked him, "Do you see anything?"

The blind man said, "I see people that look like trees walking around." Jesus touched him, and the man instantly regained his full vision.

We may not fully understand what Jesus was demonstrating with this blind man. Perhaps a partial healing only helps us see men as trees walking around. A full healing, a touch from Jesus, lets us see people with the full clarity of perfectly restored vision. Jesus worked and taught with parables and examples. This story of fully restored sight holds deep significance for us.

Jesus's first encounter with Peter shows us how God saw him. During their very first meeting at the Jordan River, John 1:42, Jesus changed Peter's name from *Simon* to *Peter*. The name *Simon* is itself a pretty good, sonorous sounding name. It means, "God hears." However, Jesus wanted Peter to recognize that it wasn't about what he thought of God but, rather, what God thought of him.

The name *Peter* means "a rock." Others saw him as an unstable, bombastic, lousy fisherman who always slept through the prayer meetings. Jesus saw this poor fisherman as a rock. Jesus saw potential in Peter while others saw only failure. Risking an unwanted theological debate, I want to give you my interpretation of what Jesus said to Peter in Matthew 16:16-19. You remember that a dialogue took place in Caesarea Philippi, a resort town north of Galilee, between Peter, the disciples, and Jesus as to whom men thought Jesus to be. Peter's answer was the right one, "You are the Christ, the Son of the Living God." This was followed by the "Blessed are you" statement by Jesus. The next statement has generated debate among religious sages and theologians for nearly two millennia: "And I tell you that you are Peter, and on this rock I will build my church (Matt. 16:18)."

The Roman Catholic Church argues that Jesus prophetically established Peter as the Rock-Pope of the church. Evangelicals see it differently. They believe Peter's confession was the rock on which Jesus would build his church. They believe Jesus was trying to say, "Peter, you're a little pebble of a rock, but on your confession of me, this Gibraltar of a Rock, I will build my church."

I have a third interpretation which I humbly submit as the correct one. I call it the Larry Titus interpretation.

Paul said that Jesus Christ is the true Head of the church. He is seated in heaven at the right hand of the Father. Evangelicals base their beliefs on a Greek text of the Scripture. However, Jesus spoke in Aramaic. This language makes no distinction between a small rock and a large rock. A rock, "cephas," regardless of the size, is a rock is a rock is a rock. It's all the same word. May I suggest that Jesus spoke prophetically to Peter and told him he was to become a "rock" and his new rock nature would determine the rest of his life's ministry?

Jesus wasn't trying to canonize Peter! Rather, Jesus was seeing Peter as the Father saw him, a rock of a man who would eventually haul in the gospel net, full of three thousand souls on the Day of Pentecost. *Jesus saw in Peter who he was to become, not who he already was or had been.* God sees the future of a person, but, sadly, we too often see only a person's present and past.

How Do You View Others?

I want God to give us "Son-glasses." No, I haven't misspelled the word. I called them "Son-glasses" because I want men to begin seeing people through God's lenses. I want to transform lives, and I want to transform yours! I want to clearly see others and speak into their lives words of encouragement, value, and prophetic affirmation. It would be a shame for me to not see people as God has created them. All around us there are people who have latent talents and abilities that could explode and grow far past anything we can imagine. But these talents and abilities will lie dormant unless someone tends to the people who hold them. These people *must* be told how special they are in the eyes of God. They must understand how God made them. I want to speak up to them, not down to them. They need someone to call them "Rocky." And I'd love to be that someone. Why? After decades of ministry, I have seen people change, I have seen chains cast off, and I have seen suffering thrown off like an old piece of clothing after people agree with God as to how they were made. I encourage you to bring this about in your own life and then in the lives of others.

At a recent men's breakfast in Hanover, Maryland, I had all the men bring Son-glasses with them. I wanted them to have the ability to see others as rocks, just as Jesus saw Peter. I encouraged the men to see other people as God does—diamonds to be extracted from the coal and gold to be refined from the ore.

When we see clearly—as God does, through his Son-glasses—we see phenomenal potential in others, and we see the compassion of God working through their lives and out into the world.

Jesus saw (and still sees!) people as they could be, as the people they can become. He selected all twelve of his disciples with this forward vision. Yet, we generally see people in terms of their histories. We see men as trees walking, not as rocks from which the foundations and walls of the church will be built. We tend to see people for all their problems, imperfections, weaknesses, idiosyncrasies, and failures. Jesus sees people as God originally created them to be, then calls forth the beauty of their true selves for all to see. We habitually view others in a dimly lit and limited way. When we see clearly—as God does, through his Son-glasses—we see phenomenal potential in others, and we see the compassion of God working through their lives and out into the world.

How fervently I believe this, and I tell you this with great excitement! We must see others as God sees them!

There is not a person alive without massive "holes." Each one of us has flaws and imperfections. There are no impeccable people on this globe and there won't be until we are at last in the presence of God. But in spite of all our failings and faults, God has chosen to use us and deposit his Spirit within us. More than that, God has designed and created us to be special in him. God looks past our temporary failings and sees us for what we can become. He calls us to see others in this way as well.

I challenge you to begin viewing people through Son-glasses. Take off your critical glasses and put on affirming glasses. See potential and encourage it. Don't speak down to people, especially your wife and children, by calling them names, deriding them, degrading them, criticizing, or maligning them. Don't let yourself criticize people inwardly or under your breath. You don't have to say something out loud for your thoughts to have a detrimental effect on your attitudes and actions—others feel your vibes.

It's not enough to simply rid yourself of negative attitudes toward people. We must also encourage them, promote them, and prophetically affirm them. God wants you to be that "Jesus" in their life who says, "You're a rock, and God is going to use you mightily in his kingdom."

Through the years I have watched men change, literally before my eyes, as I have spoken positively and prophetically into their lives. I've seen men with little confidence begin to thrive and grow as they were given constant encouragement, edification, and coaching. I've seen them change from glory to glory and come into focus as beautiful and anointed people. I pray that when I get to heaven, I will see a line of men as far as the eye can see who have become all that Jesus intended them to be because of my positive influence in their lives. In the meantime, I will continue to see myself as *awesome* and you, my friend, as *incredible*!

Chapter 2

Your Mind

IT'S ALL IN YOUR HEAD

F OR YEARS I TOLD myself I couldn't remember numbers. My brain functioned accordingly, and, indeed, I didn't recall numbers. The brain is a magnificently complex computer. It can receive instructions and then execute the coded programs. By repeating to myself that I couldn't memorize numbers, I was coding myself for number amnesia, and I got the expected result.

But one day I began changing my own source code. "You can remember numbers, all kinds of numbers." Suddenly telephone numbers, checkbook numbers, statistics, social security numbers, zip codes, and even Bible references became easy for me to memorize.

Men routinely tell me they can't remember names. "I can remember faces, but I just can't remember names." Congratulations! As long as you tell yourself you can't remember names, you never will. As soon as someone tells you their name, your brain will say, "I can forget that. After all, you told me years ago I couldn't remember names, so to this day I've followed those instructions." When you tell your brain you can't remember Bible verses, you won't. Programmers will say, "Well, of course, 'garbage in and garbage out.'" When you feed your brain bad code or instructions, you'll get a bad result.

The Worst Things We Can Tell Our Brains

Memory lapses are inconvenient and embarrassing, but there are other more damaging and sinister consequences when you tell your brain to believe statements like "I'm not smart," "I'll never succeed in my profession," "I won't live long," "People don't like me," "I'm ugly," "I'm not worthy," "God doesn't like me," "I'll never be financially successful."

We can blame our peers, insensitive adults we encountered growing up, our parents, and even the devil for these beliefs. But men, listen to me! You can be your own worst enemy when *you* tell yourself negative and demeaning things. What *you* tell yourself is far more destructive than what others can say to you.

The Power of the Mind

I am writing to you as a father and a coach, and I want to build strong minds and hearts within you. I want you to know your mind has enormous power to make you or break you. It has the power to bring sickness or health to your body, which is the lowest part of your nature. Your mind feeds input into your spirit, the highest part of your nature, and influences the way you respond to God. If the mind is filled with good, godly thoughts, it will bring the body into conformity. Your heart will beat with God's, and your spirit will be wondrously sensitive to his Spirit.

Our minds believe whatever we tell them. And as soon as you believe it, you can speak it. And when you speak it, it becomes reality. In fact, even when others say negative things about you, your mind can refuse to accept this bad coding and can replace those inputs with positive and powerful instructions.

Those Sinister Thoughts

Defend yourself from those sinister thoughts bouncing about your cranium. They accuse you of being nothing more than what you were in the past. Don't listen to them and don't believe them! These thoughts relate to our fallen nature and invariably come with mental suggestions that we've sinned too much to warrant God's grace. In other words, we'll never change.

Ideas about my past identity can determine how I see myself today. Instead of identifying who I am as a brand new creation in Christ, I identify myself according to my pre-Christ days. The danger of these mental suggestions is that my past identity then determines my future course and is always destructive.

So, here's your strategy, and it comes from that great spiritual tactician, Paul. He reminds us "...if anyone is in Christ, he is a new creation; the old has gone, the new has come!" 2 Corinthians 5:17. This is how you should think of yourself. This is your new paradigm.

This same truth is revealed in so many verses of the Bible that it should have soaked into the hollow place above my neck by now. Here are just a few:

- I have been crucified with Christ and I no longer live, but Christ lives in me. The life I live in the body, I live by faith in the Son of God, who loved me and gave himself for me. (Gal. 2:20)
- For you died, and your life is now hidden with Christ in God. (Col. 3:3)
- For we know that our old self was crucified with him so that the body of sin might be done away with... (Rom. 6:6)

I've heard many men say that when the devil reminds us of our pasts we can remind him of his future. That's a cute saying, but it falls short of really comprehending and applying God's truth. When Satan reminds you of your past, you need to remind both him and yourself that your past is more than just past—it's *dead*. You aren't even the same man. You're a brand new creation in Christ. You died to your old identity and have been resurrected in Christ's new life. Plus, you are not required to tell the devil anything, but you are obligated to tell yourself who you are in Christ so you can act accordingly. Paul says, "May I never boast except in the cross of our Lord Jesus Christ, through which the world has been crucified to me, and I to the world" (Gal. 6:14).

Why then, if I am a new creation, do I continue to speak as if I'm the same old man? It's obvious that I need a brain transplant, not just a lobotomy. I need to see myself as Christ sees me, as one who has been chosen in Christ before the foundation of the world. I need to speak words that accurately reflect who I am in Christ.

Think as God Thinks

Seeing myself as Jesus and the Father sees me will change my entire outlook on sin. Sure, there's always opportunity to return to sin, but I will remind myself of whom I am. I am God's child, full of the righteousness of Christ and chosen in him before the creation of the world. When I stop feeling and thinking I'm junk, I won't respond like junk. When I view myself from God's perspective, as righteous, I will respond in a righteous way. When I see myself as God sees me, my new nature takes over and my steps and my times happen within his Will.

When I view myself from God's perspective, as righteous, I will respond in a righteous way.

Scripture teaches us that when we were born into the kingdom, we died with Christ. That's a statement of fact. It also teaches us that we were raised with Christ, and we are seated with him in heaven. The Word teaches that the old man in each of us died in Christ, and, when we were raised with him we were given entirely new identities.

When you come back into your home country from a foreign trip, you cannot offer the immigration officer two passports—one showing your identity as Sam Smith and the other as Bill Jones. You're either Sam or Bill, even if both names have the same picture. Immigration will only accept one identity. So it is in Christ. You're either the old man or a new creation in Christ. You're either dead in your sins or alive in Christ. You're either trapped in the kingdom of darkness or born into the light of the kingdom of God. You're either unregenerate or regenerate. You're either a citizen of earth or a citizen of heaven. You are either living in your old identity or your new identity. Therefore, don't be confused about who you are now!

Confused Identity

As born-again believers, we often confuse our behavior with our identity. However, God doesn't get confused. Our identity in him has been established through Christ and will never change. When he disciplines us for our behavior, it's because *we are his children.* Have you ever noticed in the mall or in the grocery store that other parents don't take too kindly to your decision to discipline their child? Their attitude is "discipline your own child, not mine."

The Word teaches that God judges the unrighteous, but he disciplines his children. That's exactly how God sees you—as his child. That's your identity. In order to be his children, we must be born again. That goes for me and you and everyone else. He means for each of us to personally accept him and to accept his love and grace in a personal way. When you are born again, you acquire a new identity which establishes two important things about your relationship with God. First, God sees you 100% righteous in his Son. He sees you fully justified by your faith. You've been fully justified from the moment of new birth, and in his eyes, you never, ever sinned. God sees you as perfect in Christ. As God's perfect child, you have the freedom and complete access to come into his holy presence at any time.

Secondly, the Father and the Son reside within us by the agency of the Holy Spirit. We are empowered to live in our new identity. And heads-up here: this is where our enemy constantly works to trip us up. Satan cannot change your new identity, and he cannot rob you of your birth certificate. But he will desperately try to convince you that nothing has changed. He will make every effort to get you to *confuse your identity with your behavior.*

Satan well knows the presence and power of the Holy Spirit within us. He just doesn't want *you* to be aware of it. We know Satan delivers lies. He'll whisper the lie in your ear that you can't change your behavior. If he can convince you of that, he'll go to the next step and tell you that if your behavior suffers, you must be the same old guy you always were. New identity? Baloney.

The Word is the antithesis of lies. The Word tells us that the Spirit who raised Jesus from the dead is the same Spirit who dwells within us. This is the same Spirit found brooding over the face of the deep in the first chapter of Genesis. This is the same Spirit who came upon the prophets of old. He even came upon sinful Saul, delaying his pursuit of David and causing Saul to stop dead in his tracks and begin prophesying with the others. This is the Spirit who spoke continually through the apostles in the early church. This is the Spirit Jesus promised would guide us into all truth. This is the Holy Spirit of God, infinite in power and wisdom. If you know Jesus and are God's child, this is the Spirit who dwells in you.

"OK," you say, "So what?" Well, here's the "So what?": God wants us to fully comprehend who we are in him and, by the power of the Spirit within us, begin living like the men we really are. Remember, Satan can't steal our new identities. And again, I ask you to hear me very clearly: *We cannot reclaim our old (or former) identities!* Why? Because, the old man in each of us is dead. So, who would want to live like a dead guy?

We are often taught that we are becoming more like Jesus. Let's make a clear distinction here. We are already perfect in Christ. God is not perfecting our identity. That's been done. In Christ, our new identity is *de facto*. It's already happened, it must be described in the past tense, a done deal. God is working in us to perfect our behavior so it will *comport* with our identity. Think about this and meditate on the distinction.

Author, counselor, and teacher Bob George has written one of the definitive books on this subject. In *Classic Christianity*, Bob comments, "When you stepped out of Adam into Christ, Christ stepped out of heaven into you and made you into a new creature! Being made into a new creation does not refer to your behavior; it refers to your identity."[*]

We need to exercise the tremendous power of the Holy Spirit that now fills us. This power will crush Satan's lies. There is no need to run endless hours on a treadmill trying to gain God's approval and prove to Satan that you really are a changed person. Listen right now as the Holy Spirit tells you that you are already fully accepted by God. Your daily struggle

---

[*] George, *Classic Christianity*, 84.

with sin has absolutely no impact on your identity in Christ. This is an astounding, soaring truth that will break your chains and throw them to the floor!

Satan's Lies

So, you've blown it and engaged in sinful behavior. Satan will immediately try to tell you, "Aha! You're not worthy. You can't come back again and again for forgiveness. Nothing has really changed and you've never changed. It doesn't work. You'll always be addicted. You'll always be the rat you always were."

Satan wants you to sink into that old, habitual depression, despondency, and despair that so often results from the guilt he tries to pile on when we sin.

His agenda is to keep you from fruitfulness and the fulfillment of God's dream for your life. He seeks to keep you isolated, emotionally down, and spiritually impotent by confusing you as to your true identity. Satan lies to you and says that your sinful behavior changes God's heart towards you. Of course, this is another lie. Once you are God's child, you are always God's child.

Please take this to heart. As I said in the previous chapter, God doesn't change. He doesn't take back what he gives. He wants us to reject Satan's lies and live that uniquely healthy life in the Spirit. That's our right, our privilege—by his matchless grace.

Recently, I spoke at a conference of hundreds of church leaders. I had invited an old friend of mine who'd attended a church I pastored many years before. He arrived late, but the ushers brought him up to the front row where I was seated. The man took a seat and leaned over to me, "I shouldn't be up here," he said, looking around at the leaders and national figures seated near us. I hugged the man around the shoulders and told him, "You do belong here—you're part of my family." God does the same thing. He will always make a place for us. Once adopted, we're a dearly loved member of his family. We have a new identity in him. God has saved us each a chair, and I exhort you to go up there and sit with him.

You Are What You Think

I'm usually speaking from a microphone, and in my imagination I am snapping my fingers loudly into the mic, and I'm pulling your attention back to me. I need you to receive this word!

God has designed us in such a way that we have tremendous mental tools at our disposal. Proverbs 23:7 says, "For as he thinks in his heart, so *is* he" (NKJV). We're not talking about positive thinking here. That's the world's language. No, we're speaking about trying to run our thoughts parallel with God's as it applies to our lives. It is so fundamentally simple yet so hard to accept. As we begin to understand our identity found in the Word of God, we will be armed and strong and firmly say no to sin and yes to righteousness.

Here's a final thought on our identity in God. Not only are we empowered to change our behavior, God *requires* us to change our behavior to comport with our perfection in Christ. For God's child, it's not optional. As the most dutiful Father, he will not allow his children to behave according to their old sinful identity. But this book is full of good news, and here's some more. As we begin to see ourselves as our Father sees us and to recognize his power at work within us, the desire to make those changes will grow in our hearts. Not only do we get his identity, he gives us an incentive to flourish in his design. That's real freedom in Christ!

Thought Tools for Fixing Stinking Thinking

- Understand how much God loves you and has already invested in you.
- Begin to see yourself as God sees you—awesome and incredible.
- Expose lies that the devil or others have spoken about you which you believed.
- Be around people who are positive.
- Avoid people who talk about others in a negative or judgmental way.

- Meditate on the Word of God. Not only read it, but memorize it and ponder it.
- Think on things that are positive.

Finally brothers, whatever is true, whatever is noble, whatever is right, whatever is pure, whatever is lovely, whatever is admirable—if anything is excellent or praiseworthy—think about such things *(Phil. 4:8)*.

- Take your thoughts captive and make them obedient to Christ. See 2 Corinthians 10:5.
- Claim the mind of Christ through the promise found in 1 Corinthians 2:16.
- Refuse all forms of condemnation. Conviction is the responsibility of the Holy Spirit, but condemnation comes from man and the devil and is destructive. Read Romans 8:1.

Devi and Me

My wife and I were raised in totally different ways. Devi's parents trained her to believe she could do anything she set her mind to do. She wasn't allowed to say, "I can't." They would force her to rephrase her comments until they reflected a positive approach. Conversely, I grew up very negatively. I can't say this was the fault of my parents. But I doubted I could do anything. Even writing this book has been a challenge. Every few days I enter the whiny stage of "I can't do that," until Devi or others give me a confidence kick in the posterior so I can tackle it again. Her self-image has always been extremely high, while mine was below sea level. I've felt so low at times I could sit on a dollar bill and dangle my legs.

Some time ago in church, we heard a sermon on low self-esteem. The speaker described the traits of those with low self-esteem. In the introduction the preacher said, "Everyone has some area in his or her life in which they are insecure." I wanted to stand up and shout, "You don't know my wife, do you?" I'd have had to sit down fast before the ushers hauled me away. Although I am really just kidding, my calling in life might have been to bring a balance to Devi's optimism. I know she'll smile when she reads this, and as she does, she'll remember something wonderful about me. She's a gift.

The Age of Depression? But I'm A Child of God!

Our society has been ravaged by depression in the past few decades. Followers of Christ have also suffered the paralyzing despair and hopelessness of depression. I cannot share this word of challenge in full disclosure and authenticity without describing my own battles and eventual deliverance from the condition Winston Churchill called his "Black Dog."

In 1980, I encountered a trial so devastating it totally destroyed my self-confidence and plunged me into deep depression. Literally, I didn't smile from January until August of that dark year. It was like walking in a continuous gray cloud with no hope of the sun ever coming out. I described it as like having a thousand deaths or a thousand divorces all on the same day.

Relief from this all-consuming depression came unexpectedly. I can't tell you why it happened, but I can tell you how it happened. I was with Devi, my mom, and another woman on an elevator between the first and fourth floors of a motel in Gresham, Oregon. God pulled back the pall of depression, and I smiled for the first time in eight months. It was totally a "God-thing." I wasn't expecting it. I'd done nothing special to bring about this incredible miracle on that day. But I began to live again!

In 1980, I encountered a trial so devastating it totally destroyed my self-confidence and plunged me into deep depression.

Yet, even though I was delivered from a spirit of depression, I would occasionally struggle as it descended upon me seeking to smother and control me as before. For days at a time I would battle, not able to see one ray of hope.

I was out jogging one night in March of 1984. I was in Sarasota, Florida. I heard the Lord say, *"How long do you want to stay depressed? Do you want to be depressed for another hour, another day, another month, or another year?"*

My response was, "Now, Lord! I want to be delivered now. I don't want to be depressed for another minute."

His reply shocked me. "*Larry, I delivered you the first time on the elevator in Oregon; now it's time for you to deliver yourself. From now on, every time depression starts to set in, I want you to tell your mind that depression thoughts are not welcome and you won't receive them. You have the power to pull down mental strongholds like depression. It's your decision.*"

The Lord then reminded me of the truth of 2 Corinthians 10:5, "We demolish arguments and every pretension that sets itself up against the knowledge of God, and we take captive every thought to make it obedient to Christ."

"It's my decision…it's my decision," I began saying aloud. "I've made the decision that depression will never set in again." I ran home a free man, and I've been free to this day. Though I've been on the teeter-totter of discouraging and depressing times, depression has never overwhelmed me in that way again. Through Christ I have the power to pull down mental strongholds. Paul says in Romans 7 that the battleground is in your mind and God has called you to be the victor. As a man thinks in his mind, so is he.

I share this with you for one reason. God intervened in my life. I was his child, and he knew my suffering. He gave me the knowledge and assurance that I could pull down mental strongholds. Then he made the Word come alive to me, and I saw in 2 Corinthians 10:5 that I'd been given the tools and weapons to be a victor on this mental battlefield. My hope is to relay this great compassion of our Father for his children and to tell the depressed of his Nearness.

So, Let's Take the Garbage Out!

Take a look at the bullet list below. No, take a long look. Read each one of them and tell yourself, "It is finished." Agree with me on this! Let's make it an informal code of ethics. Let's get rid of some junk:

- I will not allow myself to speak negatively of others.
- I will not attack myself with destructive thoughts.

- I will not speak negatively about my future.
- I will not take up the offense of others.
- I will not continually dredge up my past sins and mistakes.
- I will not allow my thoughts to entertain sexual impurity.
- I will not tell myself, "I can't!"
- I will not belittle or accuse myself.
- I will not answer the question, "How are you?" with a negative response.
- I will not complain about anything.
- I will not tear down others in order to build myself up.
- I will not continually rehearse how sick I am or magnify my diseases or weaknesses.
- I will not speak of other people's dreams in a negative way.

Now run home to Father's house yelling, "I'm free, I'm free."

Chapter 3

Your Morals

THE MANY-MORALED MAN

WE HAD A DRIVING range near our house which I passed every day walking to and from school. I don't know exactly how old I was, but I know I was old enough to know better. On one sunny California day, I happened to notice the tempting sight of golf balls which had flown over the fence and lay near the road. I quickly rationalized that since they had crossed the fence they were fair game.

If you think about it, golf balls and eggs are nearly the same size. With that brilliant thought, I returned home and got an empty egg carton. My plan for picking up the golf balls and slipping them into the egg carton was working perfectly until the owner caught me. You know, there's a truth in that old saying, "You shouldn't put all your eggs in one basket." Maybe the guy who thought that up was also stealing golf balls. Anyway, the owner's angry threats terrorized me so that to this day I've never stolen golf balls again. That frightening experience helped form my morals regarding stealing and honesty.

Another youthful lesson in the immorality of lying came one day. My father asked me, "Son, do you know where that leather strap is that I use to sharpen my razor? If I find that you hid it, I'm going to use it on you." Well, he found it. Then he noticed the notch I'd accidentally cut into the leather. I was trying to sharpen his razor just like he did. I had slipped with the razor and gouged the smooth leather. Of course, like everything we tried to hide, he found it. My father proceeded to sharpen my morals about lying with the same tool he used to sharpen his razor.

I got a swift and sure lesson on the morality of keeping my word that I'd be home at a certain time but wasn't. The consequences were on time and swift and sure!

My father-in-law taught his teenage son about timeliness. When Devi's teenage brother didn't come in at the time promised, Dad merely got in his son's bed, ready to turn back the covers when the culprit made his tardy appearance. Talk about effective!

The moral expediency of parental obedience was deeply impressed on my posterior as a young boy. My mother told me not to go outside and play after church but to remain inside the sanctuary with her. It was clear to me she didn't fully appreciate how much fun the front step rails really were. They doubled perfectly as monkey bars for little kids. Nor was she remotely sensitive to the fact that all the other kids were playing on them. When she discovered I had disobeyed, she made a promise during the car ride home that I desperately hoped she'd forget. I talked a lot on the way home, hoping to distract her. Well, no use. Her memory proved incredibly accurate, and today, fifty-five years later, so does mine. I'll never forget my trip to the bedroom as she applied the old board of education to the seat of my understanding.

My convictions on respecting authority came when my dad, who was a vineyard foreman, asked me to pick up a grape stick and hand it to him. I told him, "Get it yourself." So he did. Then after he got it I got it! Nonchalantly walking over to the stick and picking it up, he then used it to prevent any possibility that I might run the risk of being "spoiled" by not "sparing the rod." To this day I've never, ever told anyone to "Get it yourself."

What student hasn't cast a sinful gaze at the next kid's test to see his answers? And what about those notes on cheat sheets? My lesson on the consequences of cheating came during a test in General Science in a high school class. The teacher took away the notes stuffed in my shoe. "You know better than that. You'll have to take the test again." I cannot tell you how dirty I felt. And sitting in the side room with a couple of other cheaters retaking the test reinforced the seriousness of my sin.

Good morals are taught by parents, pastors, teachers, coaches, civil authorities, friends, books, and a host of other sources. Paul teaches us that the Law of God is written internally on our hearts, and our consciences will bother us when we sin—even before we are born again.

We're Born with a Moral Sense!

While morals are taught by life and society, a basic moral sense is hard-wired into us from birth. That doesn't mean we are born with the willingness to live morally. It merely means we intuitively have the capacity to learn and recognize moral choices. I can't be convinced that man is born basically good. I've seen too many kids to believe that. No siree, Bob! They come out of the womb as mean little rascals, manipulating their parents from the get-go. When they get to the toddler stage, they're already looking in both directions hoping not to get caught. Basically good? Yeah, right.

Honesty, integrity, keeping promises, paying bills, and faithfulness to our wives are among the many moral issues men face today (as they have been for most of human history). They require us to make decisions to say no to the wrong choices and yes to the right ones. But how are wrong and right determined? Who says what's right and what's wrong? It's simple—God does. Whether our moral barometer is from our inner conscience, the Ten Commandments, the laws of the land, the traditions of a culture, or the rules our parents established, eventually the only true gauge of what constitutes sin or righteousness comes from God. He is ultimately the only one to whom we will all report.

The Shifting Sands of Socially-Determined Morals

If society is allowed to determine moral values, those values will always have an elastic element to them; they'll always be in a state of flux. The culture doesn't have a straight rod against which to measure things, because everything in society is relative. Society's standards continually change, but God's never do. God's measuring stick, his character, as defined in the Bible, never changes. Sin is sin is sin, and the wages of sin is death (Rom. 6:23).

It might seem an impossible task to live up to God's unyielding standard, but I've got good news for you. God knew from the beginning, even before Adam and Eve transgressed, that man would not be good on his own. Man's nature is not to evolve but to devolve. That's why God decided before it all began that the only solution for man's failure was to send one more man, his Son, to remedy the sin problem forever. This is where God's view will always be at odds with the world's view. Think about an unbeliever trying to make good moral choices. He will do so in his own self righteousness. That's just not good enough. God sees every believer as perfect in Christ. We do not labor under guilt to make good moral choices. The "guilt program" is Satan's. Instead, we are empowered by the Spirit within to make the moral choices that confirm the Father's image of us. Remember, he can't even see us as sinners!

Know What the Bible Calls Sin

According to 1 Corinthians 6:9-10 (NASB), God calls sin the worship of idols or other gods, cursing, the breaking of the Sabbath, disobedience to parents, murder, adultery (sexual sin by married couples), stealing, accusing people falsely, coveting others' possessions, fornication (sexual sin of any kind by unmarried people), homosexuality, effeminate behavior, drunkenness, slandering and swindling. In Revelation 21:8 and 22:15 sinful practices also include magic arts and lying. And to cover everything else that should be included, in James 4:17 God says, "Anyone, then, who knows the good he ought to do and doesn't do it, sins."

There are a lot of other sins listed in the Bible, but these should provide a good "not to do" list. Remember, sins are not mistakes but deliberate choices. Mistakes may not require repentance, but sins do. Also remember: as a child of God, you are empowered to make the positive choices which will bring your behavior closer on a day-by-day basis to the perfection you already have in Christ.

Sexual Immorality (the Sins of the Fathers)

Guys, our moral character is far more than only our sexual conduct. In fact, in my opinion, the most important part of a man's character is his ability to keep his word. When we say that we'll be somewhere at a certain time, we need to be there and be on time. When we say we'll return a neighbor's hammer, we have to do it. But let's be real here and get this out in the open. There is no sin so devastating, guilt-ridden, secretly-conducted, and deeply-addictive as sexual sin. Men, we need to look sexual sin square in the eye and confront it. I will spend most of this chapter dealing with it and sharing keys for prevailing over this noxious and devastating immoral behavior.

Let's face it. Almost without exception, sexual temptation is the biggest spiritual, mental, and emotional challenge men face. Sexual fantasies and wrong sexual thinking are ignited by pornography in all its many forms. An enormous amount of sexually-alluring material bombards men on a daily basis. It's everywhere! All forms of media use sex to sell their products. Pick up a magazine in the barber shop, turn on the Sunday game, or watch a movie. You're shown artful and seductive images of women designed to attract you. In fact, they're designed to get a lustful response!

The media bombards men with a constant show of tantalizing sexual temptation. The enticement is nearly overwhelming. I'm not talking about stepping into the trash stalls of pornographic purveyors. I'm referring to the open sexual assault that comes by walking down the street or flipping on a TV or computer.

Why, a man could backslide just walking past that well-known lingerie shop in the local mall. And who needs hardcore pornography or grimy visits to peep shows when we're constantly hammered with scantily clad women in beer ads? You think that quick review of the lingerie section in a catalogue is harmless and innocent? I know men who started down a long path of sexual sin by doing just that. Sexual sin builds on itself, and it builds quickly.

Understanding Sexual Sin

Before tackling sexual addiction, I want to discuss the nature of sexual sin. It's crucial that we see this issue from God's perspective. Listen closely! We all deal with this, and I want you someday to be teaching this to others.

In his first letter to the Corinthian church, Paul lays down a supremely important concept. God places a phenomenally high value on our bodies. God jealously claims the physical body of a believer. Paul tells us in 1 Corinthians 6:18 that, "All other sins a man commits are outside his body, but he who sins sexually sins against his own body."

God's Ownership of Our Bodies

When Jesus paid the ultimate price for us, he purchased not only our souls and spirits, but he also purchased our bodies. No matter what you think of your own body, God has made it a temple of the Holy Spirit! While the Spirit gives life to our spirits, he dwells in the container of our bodies. Just as God allowed nothing profane in the Old Testament temple, He will not allow sexual sin to profane our bodies. Imagine it! Your body is the temple of the Holy Spirit. I find this absolutely astounding and ask you to further consider that Adam was created in the image of God and given a body. Jesus came in a body, and he suffered horribly in his body. He was resurrected in a body the disciples could see and touch. They could see where the nails had been driven into him! And in this now eternal body, Jesus will forever live and come back to the earth.

Men, as believers, we will be raised from the dead or translated at Christ's return. As I write this, I marvel at God's plan. Our bodies will be changed into an eternal form exactly like the eternal body of Jesus. In fact, Paul says that our bodies don't even belong to us any longer. They were purchased by Jesus and belong to him. That's why this issue of sexual sin is so important! When we profane our bodies with sexual connection outside of marriage, we ignore and negate the purpose for which our bodies were redeemed. Our bodies are not meant to be "one" with sexual partners outside of marriage. They are not meant to be profaned by illicit sexual and immoral behavior. Quintessentially, sexual sin violates God's claim on our bodies as his holy temple.

Sin in the 21st Century

Since the Garden of Eden, the devil's tactics have never changed. The problem is that we put 21st-century spin-doctoring on sin. Here's some of the spinning:

- "Sin is relative."
- "Sin is not necessarily sin for everyone."
- "Who are you to judge?"
- "God is a God of love and would never send anyone to hell."
- "That's not as bad as a hypocritical Christian."

It's amazing how creative we can become when excusing and scape-goating our way around dealing with sin. We take clear definitions of sin according to the Word of God and twist them to fit our own rationalizing interpretation. I call that "The New Reversed Version" of the Bible.

I'm old fashioned enough to believe that the Bible is the infallible Word of God and will never change regardless of the modern revisions. The Bible is the plumb line of truth for everything else. Our purpose should not be to change the Bible so that it conforms to modern society or

The Bible is the plumb line of truth for everything else.

our personal situations. Rather, our purpose should be to see the culture change until it conforms to the Word of God. You can be sure that I'll always stick with this "old-fashioned" belief.

A hospice patient knows it as he questions the life choices of heavy smoking, a life-controlling addiction which resulted in incurable disease and great loss and pain for his loved ones. A young woman who opts for abortion knows it. A young girl and the baby taken from her and given up for adoption know it. Carriers of STDs know it. *Sin has a price.*

As anyone who has swept his eyes stealthily over the images of bare skin in pornographic magazines can bear witness to, the visual images secretly obtained, unless repented of, will wrap their icy tentacles around a person's psyche until they produce death—of integrity, of conscience, of honest relationship, of, potentially, eternal souls. Jesus's admonition that the thief comes to steal, kill, and destroy is as apropos today as it ever was, especially in the area of sexual sin. Many seemingly great, godly, character-filled men have fallen into the trap of sexual sin. Believe me, the pit is deep and the shovels to dig out are few.

Sexual Sin is Nothing New

Did you forget that that sex was God's idea? What an idea, eh? I wish I had more ideas like that. God's purpose was for sex to be between two people, a man and a woman I might add, so those two people would be bonded together in the cords of marriage. That's the way it started out. God brought Adam and Eve together then said, "Go for it." Mankind has been going for it ever since. The problem is not sexual activity. It is in man's attempt to enjoy sex outside the boundaries of marriage. Sex in magazines, sex with ourselves, sex on the internet, sex with someone besides our wife, sex with a person of the same sex, and sex in movies are all illegitimate forms of sexual release. God wants us to have sexual activity in ways which honor him. He doesn't want us to have sex with the wrong person or in the wrong way. God is amazingly and purposefully narrow-minded about sex. He wants us to know the fulfillment he intended for it by having sex only with a wife, and, for the unmarried man, he wants us to wait on sexual activity until that bond has been established. Since God is the creator of sex, we can be certain he's clear on how he wants it to function.

There's Really Nothing Mysterious about Lust

Lust is a fleshly appetite. When it goes beyond submission to God's control, it can make us slaves to sin. Lust results when a normal desire for sexual satisfaction moves outside the covenant boundaries of marriage and into the forbidden fruit of illicit passions.

Lust results when we start looking over the fence into someone else's yard. We discover in 2 Samuel 11, that lust occurred in the heart of King David when he looked over the fence into Bathsheba's bathtub. Not only did David see her taking a bath, but he visually imagined what it would be like if he were in the tub with her. The fact that Bathsheba was another man's wife didn't seem to concern him.

For King David, the visual Bathsheba-bathing-feast led to a gluttonous "feast" of adultery. David's effort to cover up his sin of adultery led him to scheme the death of Uriah, Bathsheba's husband and one of David's most loyal soldiers. Notice how the initial desire for Bathsheba led to lust and this lust led to death. The consequences of David's sin led to the death of the child he conceived with Bathsheba. As well, Nathan the prophet declared to David that his sin would bring trouble on his entire household. It was indeed the case, with rape, murder, and intrigue rampant throughout his family and kingdom. Sexual sin might be done in secret, but it always has visible and profound costs. Certainly, as in all sin, "if you play, you pay."

I encourage you to memorize James 1:14-15. The text is a great summary of cause and effect. "But each one is tempted when, by his own evil desire, he is dragged away and enticed. Then, after desire has conceived, it gives birth to sin; and sin, when it is full-grown, gives birth to death."

Every man would be well advised to give a hearty, "Amen!" to that statement.

Where to Start?

OK, I can hear you saying, "Larry, I know you're on the money about sexual sin. *But what do I do?*"

I suppose I could try to shock you into avoiding sexually charged situations by telling you stories of men who've had their lives indelibly marked by sexual sin. Pastors, professors, poachers, pundits, philanthropists, physicians, panhandlers, politicians, pupils, and parents have all fallen prey to this deceptive enemy. Sexual sin is an equal-opportunity destroyer.

You all have heard sex statistics similar to these: "80 % of business men have..." "70% of pastors have..." "75% of all husbands are..." "65% of all Christian men have..." Statistics such as these are sobering and can be a good starting point to help men see the seriousness of the problem. But statistics and stories alone can never provide sufficient strength or motivation to change.

Or I could expose you to the written anonymous testimonials of all the faceless, first-name-only men who were able to escape the powerful trap of sexual addiction. More often than not, their stories will also include practical truths that helped unlock the chains holding them in bondage. The point is, if the vulnerable brother can change, so can you. Testimonies can be very encouraging and helpful. Praise God for the men who have had the courage to share their failures for the sake of seeing other men set free from theirs!

Another generally ineffective technique tries to "guilt" men into correcting their sexual sins. If enough self-righteous preachers or judgmental church members can dangle men over the threat of eternal fire long enough, the scare factor might induce change. The fact is, however, that the thrill-um, chill-um, scare-um tactics of fire and brimstone preaching may induce a temporary delay in pursuing the forbidden fruit, but it's never long-lasting. In fact, such efforts can cause sexual sin to be more alluring. Using fear to evoke change means fear is always in play. It must be used over and over. Even then, fear and condemnation never produce lasting positive results. Fear can produce fear, but never liberty.

Lastly, there's the "grunt" method. It's endorsed by dominant, choleric personality types who believe the solution to overcoming sexual sin is to simply try harder. Grab those boot straps and pull yourself up and out of the sin! Tell yourself long enough and loud enough you can make it and you will. Be the little engine chugging up the hill chanting, "I think I can, I think I can, I think I can," and eventually you will. Those strong, disciplined leaders forget that most men in the population don't share their personality traits. Most guys don't even have straps on their boots with which to pull themselves up. The "grunt" method might seem to work work well for the highly disciplined person but is a dismal failure for every other personality type.

In Case Those Don't Work

There is an almost overwhelming amount of guilt and shame associated with sexual addiction among believing men. As men move beyond brief interludes with pornography or graphic material into full blown addiction, Satan has convinced us that we are too unworthy to return to God. We feel we can't ask him one more time for forgiveness. We become convinced there is no way out. We come to hate ourselves and think that God is disgusted with us. We buy into the lie that God cannot possibly love guys like us and couldn't or wouldn't even begin to consider taking us back. We have a foot in the trap set by Satan. Thus, the methods I note above don't work.

We must have a spiritual revelation! We must know how God sees us and who we are in Christ. When we are saved, we take on new natures. I'll happily pound on the table and repeat this until you believe God made you in his image and he places a high value on you—a value so high we cannot understand it. Men, we are made perfect in Christ, and, in his powerful grace and by his gracious power, we can become Teleios Men.

The Holy Spirit is our powerful ally. His mission is to change our thinking about ourselves and empower us to change our behavior to reflect our new identity in him. There are indeed necessary and helpful steps to experiencing freedom in this area. But the power of these steps is gained only after we understand how God sees us and how we should subsequently see ourselves.

Two Elements of Sexual Freedom

I've met men who have experienced true sexual freedom in Christ. These fellows seem to have a couple of things in common. They have the activity of the Holy Spirit present in their lives and they have a willingness to be open, vulnerable, and accountable. There are several other common personality patterns in those holding true sexual freedom, but these seem to be most critical.

The Work of the Holy Spirit

The work of the Holy Spirit is to guide us into all truth. If you find yourself trapped in sexual addiction and yet your heart genuinely cries to be free, the *first* thing to do is ask the Spirit to reveal the Father's absolute, unequivocal love and acceptance of you, his child. God is not mad at you or disgusted with you, and he is not reluctant to take you back. The Word teaches us that nothing can separate us from the love of God. We have every right to ask him to confirm in our hearts that we are his children. We can fully expect he will do so when we ask.

The lie of sexual addiction is that there is no hope because we cannot choose to be free. The Word teaches we have been set free already from the power of sin from the moment that we were born again. Satan wants you to believe that you have no power to get out. God wants you to see that you are, in fact, fully empowered to get out. The power of the Spirit already resides within you. If you begin to see who you are in Christ, you will begin to see clearly that sin is no longer your master.

Transparency

Once men are awakened to how God sees them and start changing how they think of themselves, they need to take another big step. They must absolutely begin a life of greater transparency. Those who are truly successful in breaking out of sexual addiction make a choice to leave their lives of secrecy, to expose their sins, and to embrace openness, accountability, and vulnerability. They step up and courageously reveal whatever they've been hiding. They come out of the closet in the good sense. In fact, they open the door of their closets and flip on the lights. You see, these men tire of their hidden lifestyle choices and decide to no longer live a lie. They take heroic measures and make sure shame and guilt no longer control their choices. They are so moved by their recognition of Father's love that they were willing to face the addiction head on and come clean with those who love them. They are finally moved to recognize the resident power of the Spirit within them. They begin taking the steps and making the choices that will lead them to living as the persons they already are in Christ.

Sexual Sin Can Hide

A man can continue his life as a father, parent, church leader, and civic patron but keep a dark hidden relationship with sexual sin and addiction. He cannot and will not find deliverance until he is willing to openly admit and confess his sin and to actively seek a point of accountability with one or more of his brothers in Christ. Without openness, there is no deliverance. I have never met a man who was walking in freedom from sexual sin who didn't experience the activity of the Holy Spirit in his life and who wasn't open and transparent about his struggle.

You can win over the degradation and shame of sexual sin if you know Jesus.

Success in overcoming sexual sin can't result from your actions alone. Jesus already took action and won this fight for you. All the behavior adjustments you can make mean nothing. It all depends on who you know. You can win over the degradation and shame of sexual sin if you know Jesus. Allow him to release his life through you.

The bottom line? Only the presence of the Holy Spirit can provide both the process and the power to set you free from the chains of sexual bondage and liberate you into true freedom in Christ.

The Risk of Sexual Addiction

Those who think they are exempt or impervious to the paralyzing risk of sexual addiction should strongly consider Paul's admonition in 1 Corinthians 10:12: "So, if you think you are standing firm, be careful that you don't fall!"

Not all men actively wrestle with sexual addiction, but the possibility is always there. According to Stephen Arterburn and Fred Stoeker, 10% of all men are already in the grip of sexual addiction.[*]

The following section contains a short set of lists that will help you orient your sexual behavior back to God's way. I hope they are helpful!

So, how do you know if we are at risk of sex addiction? I've listed some signs and symptoms:

1. Claiming to be able to quit sexual activity outside of marriage whenever at will, but these actions continue.

2. Habitual viewing of pornography—in print or on videos or on the internet.

3. Hiding sexual activity, including masturbation, from your wife.

4. Development and practice of playing out sexual fantasies.

5. Regularly visiting pornographic shops, strip shows, or video booths.

6. Any practice of sexual voyeurism.

Steps for breaking sexual addictions:

1. Become consistently accountable and spiritually vulnerable to other Christian brothers and join a support group. Don't be deceived into thinking this addiction can be broken alone.

2. Be accountable to your wife. Let her know your vulnerabilities and weaknesses. Ask for her assistance.

---

[*] Arterburn and Stoeker, *Every Man's Battle: Winning the War on Sexual Temptation One Victory at a Time*, 31.

3. Read the Word. The Bible will keep you from sin. Psalm 119:11: "I have hidden your word in my heart that I might not sin against you."

4. Treat sin as God treats sin. It's sin! Don't sugarcoat sin with modifying words and call it a "mistake." Sin is a transgression. Certain descriptions of sin betray a dangerous lack of knowledge: "I fell into sin." No, you don't fall into sin. You make a deliberate decision to sin. And when you say, "I made a mistake," you're still not facing reality. Mistakes don't require forgiveness, but sin does. If it's really only a mistake you made, then there is no need to repent. But if it's a sin you committed, then you must call it what it is, sin, and repent of it.

5. Kill and Flee. In 1 Corinthians 6:18, Paul says that all sins that a person commits originate outside the body, but that *sexual* sins are against the body.

    •   That is why Paul writes in Colossians 3:5 that a person must put to death sexual sins. You don't tolerate sins, but, by the power of the Holy Spirit, you kill them! In the same chapter Paul tells you the types of behavior that you should put off and the new expression of Christ that you should put on. But when it comes to sexual sin, the command is unequivocally clear. Kill it. No ifs, ands, or buts about it.
    •   Paul wrote to Timothy to "flee the evil desires of youth" (2 Timothy 2:22). Paul was giving Timothy information he'd need in the future. He must dodge sexual temptation. The process is simple, kill sexual sins and then run for your life when you are exposed to them.

6.   If no support groups exists for sex addicts, start one. Pure Life Ministries has several excellent programs for men wanting to escape the bondage of sexual addiction. You can contact them through the internet at www.purelifeministries.org.

7.   Read Christian books by men who have been there. There are several Christian titles that you can read. They go into greater detail and provide much more information on sexual addiction than I can address in this chapter.

- Dr. Ted Roberts wrote *Pure Desire*. This is an excellent book full of practical steps you can take to break this bondage. Ted's Vietnam era illustrations are worth the price of the book. His book has a great appeal to "real men."
- Stephen Arterburn and Fred Stoeker authored two inspiring books, *Every Man's Battle* and the companion *Every Man's Challenge*. As Dr. Jack Hayford says, they provide "an arsenal of resistance."
- Steve Gallagher offers great advice for men in his book, *At the Altar of Sexual Idolatry*. I highly recommend it.
- Dr. Jack Hayford wrote a trilogy of books describing men's biggest challenges and the biblical answers. *The Anatomy of Seduction, Fatal Attractions,* and *Sex and the Single Soul* are outstanding resources for men who are serious about change.

Safeguards for Preserving Healthy Sexuality

Here are a few suggestions on how to safeguard a healthy, happy, and blessed sex life:

1.   Make your wife your number one priority and the only sexual attraction in your life.

2.   Practice regular discipline of your eyes and flesh.

3.   Do nothing in secret. (Luke 12:2-3)

4.   Confess your past sexual sins to someone you can trust and to whom you can remain accountable. (James 5:16)

5.   Be sensitive and not condemnatory to those who fall lest you likewise fall. Extend to others the same grace that Jesus has given you. (Gal. 6:1)

6.   Pursue righteousness. It is not enough to flee sin, the negative aspect, but you must also pursue righteousness, the positive aspect. (2 Tim. 2:22)

7.   Be cautious about who you hang out with and stay away from bad influences. Avoid the "harmless" sexual jokes and banter. Choose to be around healthy Christians. (Prov. 24:1; Jer. 15:17; 1 Cor. 15:33; Ps. 1:1-2)

8.   Watch what you watch! Because men are so visual, in their minds the eye-gate is an enormous entrance for sin.

One of the most encouraging passages in the Bible is found in 1 Corinthians 6. After listing all the sins of the flesh in verses 9 and 10, Paul concludes in verse 11 by saying, "And that is what some of you were. But you were washed, you were sanctified, you were justified in the name of the Lord Jesus Christ and by the Spirit of our God."

Won't it be a wonderful blessing to be able to honestly say, "That is what I used to be!" That is precisely what God wants your testimony to be! Men, we can do this! Let's start right now.

HEALING THE
FATHER WOUND

MARK SAT IN MY office pounding on the back of the sofa and yelling, "I hate my dad; I hate my dad; I hate my dad. Why did God let me go through this? Why didn't he stop my dad from drinking?"

Mark had tried hard to keep his father in the house. He knew his mother would throw his father out if the drinking continued. But Mark's efforts were frustrated, and his father was pitched out of the home. "After that, he was never there for me. He never attended any of my football games. All the other guys had dads who came to watch them play, but he never came. I hated him for it."

There in my office, I heard it and saw it. There was real debilitating anger and pain in this young man. Men old and young have cried with me in counseling sessions as they poured out their pain over this same kind of devastation.

During a Los Angeles conference, I sat with another man whose shoulders shook with near uncontrollable sobbing. "My dad never came to any of my games, and he was unfaithful to my mother. I thought, since we lived in the same town, at least he would come to my wedding. But no, he was too busy!"

At that same Los Angeles conference, a handsome, talented, athletically-built actor and director shared, "My testimony is not the same as the other men. My dad was always there for me. He always came to my games." Suddenly, in the middle of his testimony he stopped. After a few moments of awkward silence, he said, "That's not true." Somberly, he continued, "I've been sharing that same lie for years. I didn't think Hollywood would let me into the movie industry if they really knew my background. I never had a dad. I don't even know who he is. I grew up without any male role model. No one was ever there for me."

For many men, the deepest emotional wound they will ever experience is inflicted by their fathers. I touched briefly on the father wound in Chapter One, and now I'll address this painful reality in more detail. During many years of ministry and counseling with thousands of men, I have witnessed countless moments when the lid comes off a man's capped emotions and out flows a torrent of built up anger and frustration. In most of the men, anger resulted after their abusive fathers had left serious wounds. The abuse came in many forms and was by verbal or physical abuse or a combination of both. For others, it was the hurt created by the injustice of having a disconnected dad or of not having a dad at all. In either case, the pain was real, deep, enduring, and is quite often passed to the next generation.

Fathers can wound their sons in many different ways. It might come from an absentee dad who's there physically but not emotionally. He comes home from work, turns on the television, and shuts himself off from everybody. The son sees him, but steers clear, knowing from experience that his dad doesn't want to be bothered. Attempts at conversation simply don't work. The boy learns that he cannot discuss his deepest issues and fears with his dad. Anger, frustration, and even hatred take root in the boy's heart. These emotional states deepen as time goes by, and, of course, behavior is affected by them.

Quite often, men tell me, "I know he loved me, but he just never told me. He always worked hard, but he didn't know how to show emotion." That's the common description of an emotionally-detached dad. The children vaguely recognize they are loved because they get food and shelter. It's better than nothing, but it's a poor substitute for emotional, relational love.

The emotionally-detached dad has nothing on the abusive dad—the one who exerts authority through verbal or physical abuse. Countless men describe vivid and often sickening stories of regular beatings they received from their fathers. Perhaps even more devastating is the verbal or physical abuse the wife and mother receive. The scars in the boy's heart are deep. As he gets older, the overwhelming, unresolved anger from the past adds to the frustrations of daily life. A repeating cycle of destructive behavior begins anew in another family.

There are fathers who only relate to their sons on the basis of performance. "I'll love you if you do well in sports, school, or work." Failure results in rejection. A father who values his son only for his achievements creates a boy who tries to please everyone in his life. However, the boy usually or eventually fails to really please anyone.

A hyper-competitive father is compelled to see his son win at something. But the father will say, "I could have done it better." These sons just can't win. But they never wanted to be in competition with their fathers. Whether they succeeded or failed, they simply wanted their dads to love them unconditionally.

Then there are the fathers who, through divorce, desertion, imprisonment, or other circumstances are not there for their sons at all. "I never knew my dad" is their heart-breaking cry. In many cases, the dad disappeared after the pregnancy rather than deal with the responsibility. Sometimes a divorce occurs after the son is partially grown, causing a deeply traumatic rending of the boy's heart when the father leaves the household. I've heard that within one year of a divorce, most sons no longer see their dads with any regularity even when they live in close proximity.

In all these "disappearances," the sense of rejection is real and profound. Men have virtually no sense of identity at all as a result of this kind of abandonment. Their sense of self-worth is damaged or nearly destroyed with their father's abandonment. "He didn't love me enough to stick around!" This thought deeply internalizes men. I've often held weeping men in my arms as they described memories of rejection from their fathers. Some of these guys groaned inwardly over not having a father at all.

I prayed with a young man whose father coached his hockey team. One day while the boy's team was practicing, the boy's father came out on the ice and told him he was leaving his wife, the boy's mother. The young man left the ice and hung up his skates, never to compete again. This young man eventually became trapped in drugs, disillusionment, and failure. It took a godly wife and a pastor who loved him to help him to receive healing for his crippled emotions.

Men, I am telling you stories that are real. I have seen innumerable lives marred and damaged by father wounds. Dysfunction and outright failure plagues the sons of failed fathers. In this chapter, I can't possibly explore the ramifications of father wounds in our society today. Nor can I delve into the root causes of father wounding.

Emphatically and fervently I tell you this: the failure of fatherhood is a core reason for disintegrating families, growing social epidemics, disrespect for authority, and a host of ills plaguing society at large. Sadly, the hurt and pain a father brings to his children is even now being passed from one generation to the next. We *must* stop this reproduction of pain, as we must stop other behaviors passed to those coming after us.

...the failure of fatherhood is a core reason for disintegrating families, growing social epidemics, disrespect for authority, and a host of ills plaguing society at large.

The Hurt that Hurts

Over the years, I have also counseled scores of men who were extremely abusive to their wives, children, employees, and anyone else they crossed paths with in life. Academics, social scientists, and other theorists can *talk* about this. But I have been holding weeping men and experiencing their sobs for years. I state with no hesitation that abusive men were produced in dysfunctional, abusive families. In nearly every case, there was an abusive father at the base of all this hurt and confusion.

Abused men have weak self-images and a lousy sense of worth. They are frequently described as "emotionally immature." When these men marry and have families, their lack of emotional endurance surfaces. The inevitable pressures of daily life—work, bills, marital conflict, and child rearing issues—will eventually expose their weakness. Fueled by ever-present unresolved anger over an unhealed father wound, these men revert to the same abusive behavior that they suffered at the hands of their own fathers. While the specific forms of the abuse may be different, the same insensitive, abusive spirit that they experienced growing up is in turn expressed toward their own children.

I have observed many men who want to distance themselves from their past. They don't want to deal with the father wound they carry. They decide they'll be different from their fathers. They'll do it with willpower. That's the manly way, right? So, they work hard to provide a better home and school for their kids. They work for better schooling, more opportunities, and more material things than they enjoyed in their childhoods. All the while, the anger from their own father wound simmers under the surface. Inevitably, the pressures of trying to provide a better life for the wife and kids trigger the same kind of behavior patterns they experienced.

Dad comes home tired, frustrated, and angry. The kids irritate him, and he yells at them. The wife irritates him, and he berates her. He just wants to watch some TV and be left alone. They don't understand everything he's going through to provide this fantastic life for them. As pressure builds over time, he distances himself more emotionally and often just stays away from home for longer periods. When he is home, his anger escalates at the drop of a hat, and he moves from verbal to physical abuse. The kids and wife begin to fear for their well-being when he's around. And, the same feelings of rejection, alienation, abandonment, and anger are being born in their hearts.

This scenario goes on continually in families all across our land. The devastating effects of the father wound are so massive on so many levels! So do you see? Willpower alone cannot heal the father wound that starts this cycle.

How Can the Father Wound Be Healed?

Admit that you have a father wound. You can't be healed if you deny the injury. Oddly, men often feel they are being disloyal if they admit having a father wound. Children, even grown children, want to be seen as healthy and relevant. It's often hard for a child to admit that his parents were abusive.

Understand your father's background. Your dad is repeating what he experienced as a child. Even though it's wrong and certainly not justifiable, he is likely repeating what he learned from his own abusive father. Try to learn how his father treated him!

Forgive your father. No matter what he did to you, forgive him. You've put him in a cage of revenge and bitterness. It's time to release him. Replace "I'll never forgive him" with "If God forgave me, can I do any less for my dad?" Let God deal with the sins of your father. He is the only one who truly knows your father's heart. Toss him the keys to unlock the cage. Forgiving your dad doesn't change what he did to you, but it does allow God to work. Even if your dad never has the willingness to humble himself and ask your forgiveness, you must forgive him.

Several years ago, a friend of mine was questioned by his wife in a marriage retreat about the reason for his unresolved anger. After getting angry at her for suggesting he was an angry man, he listened as she went on to say, "I think you're still angry at your dad for deserting you." She nailed it! His anger toward her was unresolved anger toward his dad. His dad had deserted his mother for another woman during his high school years. He and his siblings were forced to grow up without their father's stabilizing influence during their critical teenage years.

Several years later, his dad died. While most of his siblings refused to go to the funeral, my friend decided to attend it with two of his sisters.

Those who have been deeply wounded will often wound their own family members and others.

When he walked into the viewing room and saw the man who had deserted him years earlier, his heart broke. Prompted undoubtedly by the Holy Spirit, he walked over to the casket, placed his hands on his dad's chest and began to talk to him. "I forgive you, Dad, for never being at any of my games. I forgive you, Dad, for leaving my mom for another woman. I forgive you, Dad, for never teaching me about sex. I forgive you, Dad, for never being there for me." With that, he said it felt like all the anger had left his body. He didn't realize at the time that his anger toward his wife also vanished. Incredibly, his anger toward everyone else was gone as well. If you were to meet him today, you'd never suspect he had been an angry man. He's the most gentle, mild-mannered guy you could meet. His father wound was totally healed.

Healing for Those We've Hurt

Those who have been deeply wounded will often wound their own family members and others. Generational wounding can be and must be stopped! Even when we have been seriously wounded, we must take ownership for our own anger, verbal or physical abuse, performance-based demands, abandonment, or controlling behaviors. If our family members have suffered because of the emotional or physical abuse we've put them through, it's imperative that we reverse our actions and seek emotional and relational healing and reconciliation.

Mending Damage We've Caused Others!

Be honest. Appraise the pain you have inflicted on others. Stand up and admit it, not fearing consequences and understanding how you'll hurt these people more and more if you don't stop. If you really aren't sure if you've hurt them, ask them. I'm sure they'll be much more honest than you'd like.

Ask their forgiveness. A dad who says, "I'm wrong, please forgive me," brings more healing than can be imagined. You can't undo the past, but an apology can start an astonishing healing process.

Forgive yourself. After you've repented and sought forgiveness for any injury you have caused your family members, you must forgive yourself. Browbeating yourself is not only counterproductive but also dangerous. Self-condemnation will keep you in a prison you build for yourself.

Sometimes a personal story touches our lives in places that mere principles can't reach. Therefore, I have asked Larry Lee to write his own story.

Larry came into our lives when he was sixteen years old and will remain in relationship with us until "death do us part"—and, by God's saving grace, for eternity.

Here's Larry's story:

My mother died in 1968 at the age of forty-eight. She drank herself to death. She was an epileptic, and, over time, the alcohol wore her system down. One day she collapsed onto the floor of the small, two-room house she was living in and just died—completely alone. I was sixteen and living in my third foster home in five years when I received the phone call from my aunt telling me of my mother's death. My two sisters, a few years younger than I, were living with my aunt in foster care as well.

Five years earlier, neighbors had alerted the child welfare authorities in our state. They were concerned about us and the drunken lifestyle of my mother and her current husband. By the time the state stepped in, the two of them were consuming at least a case of beer and three to four bottles of cheap wine every day. I don't remember a time in those years when they weren't either drinking or drunk. After the authorities removed us from the home, my mother never overcame her dependency. We were never returned to her care before she died. I hadn't seen her for over a year when the news came.

Of course, they had a circle of friends living in the same lifestyle, and routinely exposed us—the kids—to some rough situations. There were often adult parties in the home with people in various stages of undress at all hours. It was not uncommon for me to come downstairs in the morning to find total strangers passed out on the living room furniture in indecent and compromising positions.

Those images are still emblazoned in my memory.

Many times in those years, we would go into town with my mother and her husband and sit in the restaurant portion of a local establishment while they would spend a few hours in the bar. People find this hard to believe, but at the age of twelve, I often drove my mother's 1948 Chevrolet or her husband's 1960 Impala the eight miles to our house outside of town because they were just too drunk to drive. And I did this on many occasions in the dead of night. Of course, the neighbors became increasingly more alarmed as the behavior of my mother and her husband grew more outrageous.

When the state finally stepped in, the question arose, "Where would they send us?"

My sisters and I went to live with my aunt. She and my uncle had a small Pentecostal church outside of town. Every year they had a summer church camp, and I had a genuine salvation experience at the age of nine in one of those camps. Because we had attended there every summer, it seemed natural we should be sent there by the state for foster care. As I grew older, however, they would not allow me to participate in school sports or attend a school dance. It was the "come out from among them and be ye separate" mentality so prevalent in old-line Pentecostal circles. After a while, I couldn't take it any longer and began my journey through four other foster homes up through my senior year in high school.

My mother was actually married and divorced five times that I know of. She was among the youngest of eleven children and was a free spirit to say the least. She had a good heart but was always drawn to sitting at the bar in one of the local taverns. I was regularly taking care of my sisters by the time I was eight years old. I would cook macaroni and cheese or some other simple meal. Sometimes I just made sandwiches. My mother would often send me to the corner grocery store to pick up a few groceries on credit. The owner would let her charge until she got her welfare check, and then she'd pay down the bill. I cannot remember a time between husbands when we weren't on welfare.

I didn't know my real father. However, I learned from my aunt after my mother's death that he had actually abandoned my mother while she was two days in the hospital after my birth. They never married, and he just disappeared. With the exception of the last man she was married to, the only memories I have of my mother's other husbands are the vague recollections of them coming and going. Alcohol was always a big part of those relationships, and none of these men was ever a father to me.

You can imagine that by the time I was in high school there was a root of anger growing deeply into my soul. I wasn't into drugs in those days and only dabbled in some drinking. I didn't smoke and was fairly athletic. You could say I was a straight kid, clean cut, and all that. But, by that time, I had suffered so much injury at the hands of adults I wasn't going to let anyone tell me what to do. I would stand up to anyone and was prepared to fight at the drop of a hat. I was a big, strong kid and could hold my own. Even with my emotional injuries, I was gener-

ally respectful of adults until they tried to speak into my life. That's where I'd draw the line. This was the reason for five foster homes in seven years. People just didn't know how to handle me or my volatility. My convictions about God were firm, but if serving him meant submitting to people in authority, I wasn't having any of it.

Looking back on that period of my life today, I realize I was completely covered over in shame. I felt the shame of being a welfare kid. I felt the shame of having to deal as an eight-year-old with the owner of the corner grocery. I felt shame in every school activity because if my mother or her husband did show up, they had always been drinking, and you could easily smell it on them. I felt shame at not having a father in every event where fathers were part of the fun. I felt shame at being exposed to adult debauchery of all kinds and for having the seeds of lust planted in my mind as a result. I felt shame during my high school years when I had to explain that I lived in a foster home. There were several of them. The kids who knew me in high school also knew I was always on the move, and this was shameful to me. Shame in my life was the fuel that fed my anger. While I could not have identified it in those days, today I realize I also had a deep and growing anger at the injustices in my life.

I was fortunate to live with a local doctor and his wife during my senior year. Their home did demonstrate to me a better way of life. Unfortunately, I was so filled with anger I was not able take advantage of any direction they might have given me. I remained on the outside of life looking in. I was such a strong personality, always on the offense, that at the end, the doctor's wife was glad to see me go. During my first quarter of college, she sent me a letter which read in part, "We're happy we were here to offer you a home last year. Now that you're gone, we don't feel there is any more we can do for you. Please look to God as your father from now on." I don't have to tell you how that felt.

But, I was also very fortunate to meet a young couple in my hometown in the summer before my senior year. They had come to take over a small church, and their youthfulness, exuberance, and energy just drew people to them. I had a Christian friend in school, and I'd attend his church with him once in a while. He invited me one night to go with him to see this young couple and sit through one of the evening services in their church. I was instantly captivated by the all-embracing love that exuded from them.

Larry and Devi Titus were a godsend to me. I was a tornado about to enter their lives. I'm one of the very first of the eighty or so guys who have lived with them over the years. And, while they had a tremendous impact on me in the early years of our relationship, I was never really willing to completely submit to Larry's leadership or to God through his ministry. I just had too much unresolved anger and pain to let anyone really get below the surface with me. Fortunately, in the thirty-seven years we've known each other, they never gave up on me. Larry has prayed for me, ministered to me, bled with and for me, and been the only father figure I've ever really known. I often say that I personally own at least one square inch of the gray hair on his head.

I was in college for two years and had absolutely no idea what I was doing there. I changed majors a half dozen times and could never really settle down. I was totally unprepared to make a decision about my future. Not only was I unwilling to receive any adult input other than from Larry and Devi, but also I continued to need years of solid parental mentoring.

I was so angry and ashamed of my past. I decided one day that if I could just get married and start a family of my own, I could fix all those painful and shameful experiences. I could paint my own canvas, create the family I never had, be the dad I always wanted to have, and, with my happy bride, chart the course for our future filled with hope for a better life. With that in mind during my two years in college, I asked four or five girls if they would marry me. Fortunately for them, they said no.

I decided to leave college and return to my home town. Back in Larry's church, I found a person who agreed to marry me. So, I was married at the ripe old age of twenty-one. Six months into our marriage, I had second thoughts about the commitment, wrote a bad check, and took off for Hawaii. I ran out of money in paradise in about a week and had to ask someone on the mainland to buy me a plane ticket to get back. Even though I came back, I was angry about making a commitment to marriage, and I began a long pattern of verbally abusing my wife.

Our three daughters were born in the early years of our marriage. While having kids offered some diversion from our marital problems in the beginning, my wife was continuing to work full time, and I didn't have the credentials to find a meaningful job. I went through all kinds of low-level jobs. The knowledge that she was doing better than I was in the workplace, coupled with the knowledge that everyone else also knew she was doing better, just added to my anger. I was tough on my kids and verbally destructive to my wife. We were separated a few times in those years but would keep trying to make it work. All the while, the anger kept bubbling below the surface, and I continued in my unwillingness to let anyone speak into my life.

I finally landed an entry-level job in the significant industry in my home town. I started feeling better about myself, but it was no time until my need to control my environment and make everything perfect began to spill over into the workplace. I would explode in anger when people wouldn't cooperate with me on the job. This happened with increasing frequency. One day the manager called me into his office and said, "I'm concerned that you're having a nervous breakdown." I tried to tone it down, but the pressures of work, kids, bills, and marital issues made home the new arena for explosive fits of rage.

I made some moves in my industry and, in 1988, started my own business. It was another thought process in which I surmised that I could resolve my frustrations and anger issues if I could just gain control of my own destiny. If I could build a business and create profitability for myself, I could fix everything: take the pressure off my wife and kids, validate my manhood, and build for the future. I could even, I reasoned, "invest in the kingdom of God." I started to work out of my basement, and, early on, had some success.

It was when I moved out of the basement, took an office, and began to hire a few people that the old patterns began to surface again. Within a few years, I had developed a consistent pattern of violently verbally abusing all my employees. I managed through fear, intimidation, yelling, and screaming. Eventually, I even destroyed all my customer and vendor relationships. Through a series of emotional and sometimes sinful choices, I found myself over one million dollars in debt. As well, my marriage was in serious trouble with constant arguing and fighting over money.

I had remained a consistent church attendee all this time but was never willing to submit to a process which would deal with the anger issues that I'd carried since childhood. In 1995, the Lord began to speak to me about facing this problem, but I just kept tuning him out. I refused all real accountability to spiritual leadership and felt that if I kept giving financially surely the Lord would understand. However, I just kept going deeper into debt.

By this time, my marriage was completely on the rocks, and my teenage kids were terrified of me. The moment my car came into the garage, they'd head for their rooms to stay out of my way. I had a violent argument with my wife after coming home one night in 1997 and managed to destroy about a thousand dollars worth of porcelain on our kitchen counter. It was while I was in the emergency room getting my hand stitched up I really recognized I was heading into the emotional abyss.

I moved out of the house that week and went to live for a year in a bed and breakfast. Things really went downhill from there. I lost my marriage of twenty-five years, I lost my company, and I hurt a lot of people in the process. While I knew I had anger issues driving the destruction, I continued trying to deal with the symptoms—not getting to the root of the problem. I would pray, but my prayers were for the restoration of my perceptions about the ideal life that I had imagined back in my college days. I wasn't praying that God would deal with the anger and help me face it head on. I ended up moving to another city and spent two years going from my apartment to my office—avoiding contact with people altogether. I'd go to a church service once in a while and pray some, but to avoid dealing with my real issue, I just became a recluse. I'd talk with my kids only occasionally and had a hard time dealing with the devastation I'd inflicted on their lives.

One day, I decided God wasn't answering, and I was done with it all. It wasn't that I doubted his existence. I was just finished with his seeming injustice in my life. In my mind, I had experienced enough injustice over the years, and I was just done with it. I remember my words to the Lord very well. Sitting in my apartment, I said out loud, "You're big, and I'm little. You can do whatever you want with me. You can swat me like a fly. I don't care. But, I'll tell you what, I'm done with you." I've often visualized the Father sitting on his throne, chin in hand, listening to that. I can see him rolling his eyes, looking over to the Son, and saying, "Can you believe this guy?"

I spent the next two years on the run, literally. But, like David says in Psalm 139, "Where can I go from your Spirit?" I was in Mexico on business for another company when one morning, about 5:00, I came right out of my sleep and sat up in the bed—wide awake. I realized the Presence of God was entering my room. As the Holy Spirit completely enveloped me in that room, I began to weep uncontrollably. The love of God swept over me in waves. There was absolutely no doubt in my mind at that moment that God loved me totally, unconditionally, and without measure.

I remember choking out the words, "I don't understand why you relentlessly pursue me. I don't understand after all the carnage I've left behind, why you would continue to chase me. I don't understand how my name could be written in your book when there are untold millions whose names will not be there." I wanted him to leave me alone. But it was the beginning of a process in which God began to reveal to me the deep father wound in my life as the source of all my unresolved anger. While I wasn't ready to completely give in, that experience began a softening in my heart and an understanding that it was OK to recognize that I was wounded.

Through a series of events too numerous to detail here, God began a process of healing in my life. One day, the Lord gave me a mental picture of a pillar, or a cylinder, of white-hot fire. I remember having this conversation: "What is it, Lord?"

He said, "Larry, that's the fire of my discipline."

"What does it mean?" I asked.

"Well," he said, "I want you to walk up to that fire, wrap your arms around it, and pull it into yourself."

"That's going to hurt a lot," I said.

"More than you know," he responded.

By that time, I had come to a place where I was willing to begin the process of healing. It's critical to recognize there's healing in the Lord's discipline even though we don't often see it at the time. It started with my repentance to the Lord, and, honestly, that took a long time. God patiently brought to mind every instance of my destructive behavior in other people's lives. The second step was to repent to people, and, over the years, I've addressed numerous issues either by personal contact or with letters. Even today, an angry moment will occasionally come to mind, and I'll try to address it if I can locate the person. I definitely address it with the Lord in repentance.

All the while, through an ongoing series of instructions by the Spirit, God has been working to heal my father wound. Much of this process has been the complete restructuring of my understanding about who I am in Christ. I know today that I am God's son, totally forgiven, fully justified, and adopted into his family. It's clear to me today that he wishes to heal the effects of all the injustices of my childhood while at the same time removing the root of anger which has driven all the dysfunction in my life. No matter what we've experienced in the past, we do have to take ownership for sinful, destructive behavior.

After my repentance came a painful but illuminating process of recognizing the scope of my wounds and forgiving those who inflicted those wounds in my past.

God graciously began to define for me the exact nature of the injuries, and I was able to forgive people for the specific injuries each had inflicted on me. Most of those people have long since passed away, but it was necessary through prayer to forgive them. In doing so, I participated in the process of setting my own heart free and reclaiming the territory in my soul that anger had occupied for so long. When we forgive others, we deny the enemy that area as a foothold in our lives. The process of forgiving those who injured us sets us free.

The most painful area to deal with, of course, is the wounding I inflicted in the lives of my three daughters and their mother. I still grieve over the thoughts of the pain and results of the abuse I introduced into their lives, not to mention the trouble they experienced from suddenly having an absentee father and a mother on her own. Even though there was a growing conflict in our home, whatever sense of security there may have been vanished when I left.

As I write this today, I am not reconciled with two of my children. They experienced the same injustices at my hands that I experienced growing up. As a result of my abusive behavior, I opened a door of anger into their lives. My constant prayer is that God will bring healing to the deep wounds and sense of injustice they feel as a result of my sinful behavior toward them. I pray as well for a complete restoration of our father-daughter relationship. Only time will tell, but

I was a wounded man who inflicted wounds on others. —Larry Lee

it's my desire that through their willingness to forgive me they too will be healed, and we'll one day be together again.

I want to mention finally what I believe to be one of the greatest hindrances to being fully healed of a father wound. In my case, I was a wounded man who inflicted wounds on others. I believe I've earnestly and honestly sought the forgiveness of those I've wounded. I believe, as well, I've completely forgiven those who hurt me. I've tried to make honest reconciliation on both sides of the issue. I believe today I am, by the work of the Spirit and the love of God in my life, completely clear in my relationship with the Lord. But there are times when Satan will come around to remind me of all the unresolved carnage yet to be cleaned up. He will point to that carnage and say to me, "Hey, Larry, too much damage. It's still a mess. You can't move on with your life. Others are still hurting from your previous angry behavior. It wouldn't be right for you to be happy while they still suffer." That's a big, big lie.

We have to move on into effectiveness and fruitfulness for Jesus. There comes a time, after honestly facing and dealing with the effects of our previous behavior, when we must leave it in God's hands to orchestrate the remaining clean up. We can't do it. And if we buy into the guilt the enemy wants to throw on us, we negate all the work the Lord has done in our lives to set us free from our past. It's like having a prison cell door thrown open to an inmate who refuses to step out into freedom. We must take that step, leaving the forgiven past behind and the rest in God's hands, if we are to become everything the Lord has destined for us to be.

So, I'm moving on with the Lord. Every day I move into more freedom. It's an ongoing process. I must continue from time to time to address the vestiges of that old root of anger. Today, I'm married to an incredible woman, and I daily thank God for his grace in orchestrating her entrance into my life. God is working in us together, and she is a force in helping me continue a complete healing process. The Lord has empowered me by the Spirit to be changed. As the Psalmist says, his discipline is the way of life. Thank God for his relentless pursuit of my life and his loving discipline. It seems painful at the moment but eventually yields the peaceable fruit of righteousness.

The Blessing

Finally, I would like to relate the recent story of a young man who was very close to me during the last months of his father's life. Because his dad was an abusive alcoholic when he and his five older brothers were growing up, I have chosen to omit his true name. However, the message still comes across loud and clear. The picture is not really of the six boys and the strain of their childhood but that of the dad who in his final days made everything right.

Though "Jim" received Christ later in life, after his boys were out of the home, all six boys grew up under deep, constant emotional and physical strain, as well as the abuse of an alcoholic father. Thankfully, he and his wife had come into an intimate relationship with Christ, and he and his adult sons have experienced a tremendous relational healing.

Just before his passing, Jim dictated to his wife a blessing for all six sons.

One by one, he called them into his room. He put oil on his hands and had each son kneel before him. Then, as his wife read the blessing, he cupped each of their faces in his hands and blessed them.

The son that told me this story said the chains that had bound him for years were falling off as his father pronounced blessings on him.

Hear the words and then hear the heart-beat of a prodigal father bringing healing to his injured sons:

> To my son:
> You are a gift from God. I thank God for allowing me to be your father.
> I bless you with healing from all of the wounds that I, and others, have caused.
> I bless you with overflowing peace—the peace that only Jesus, the Prince of Peace, provides.
> I bless you with fruitfulness in life—good fruit, much fruit that remains. You are the head and not the tail, above and not beneath.
> I bless you with prosperity. You will prosper and be in good health even as your soul prospers.
> I bless you with spiritual influence, for you are the light of the world and the salt of the earth.

I bless you with success, for your meditation upon the Word of God will make you like a tree planted by rivers of water and your way will be prosperous and you will have good success.

I bless you with a greater depth of spiritual understanding and a closer walk with your Lord. You will not stumble or falter, for the Word is a lamp unto your feet and a light unto your path.

I bless you with pure and edifying relationships in life.

I bless you with abounding love enabling you to minister God's comforting grace to others.

You are blessed, my child. You are blessed with all spiritual blessings in Christ Jesus. Amen!

With Love,

Your Father

Jim's words help us understand the real heart of a Teleios Man. The ability to deal with things so deeply and emotionally painful is the root of all true spirituality. There is nothing that would qualify you more as a completed, finished man in Christ than the ability to be contrite, broken, and humble. God says in Psalm 51:17, "…a broken and contrite heart, O God, you will not despise."

To be a true Teleios Man, we must understand that the way up in God is to get down, that we must humble ourselves to the place of brokenness and service. That's the same way to be great before our wives and families: humble ourselves and sacrificially serve them. We know we have succeeded as Teleios Men when our Lord, our wives, and our families all see daily signs in the choices we make that we consider them more important than ourselves. When they do, we're experiencing his completion.

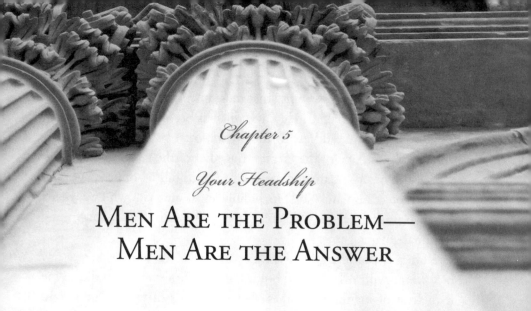

Chapter 5

Your Headship

MEN ARE THE PROBLEM—
MEN ARE THE ANSWER

YOU'VE HEARD THE FUNNY and fictitious story of St. Peter telling all the men recently arrived in heaven to go over and stand in one corner of the Celestial City. All the men responded with the exception of one timid, little henpecked guy.

"Why are you standing over here by yourself instead of with the other men?" Peter queried.

"Because this is where my wife told me to stand," said the little guy.

Then there's the old joke that over time has morphed into a myriad of different forms. The openers generally go something like, "What are the only two words you'll ever need to know to have a happy marriage?" or "We've never had a fight in twenty years. And every time my wife wants to start a fight I only have to say two words." Whatever the openers, men always laugh at the punch line, "Yes, dear!"

The humor in these jokes comes from the ring of truth in them. The laughter isn't always a laugh of amusement; it's sometimes one of nervous recognition. Men intuitively recognize that women can be very dominant from time to time in many if not most marriage relationships. In their heart of hearts, however, men also often recognize the weakness of their own headship which leads to this domination. There are, of course, exceptions, but since less than 5% of men are strong choleric (natural leadership personalities) and nearly 70% of men are laid-back "good ol' boys," there is a strong possibility that most men find it difficult to rise to their headship potential.* These days, this has become a touchy subject, but I'm not shy about addressing touchy subjects.

In my opinion, one of the greatest tragedies of the fall is that through the inception of sin, Adam abdicated his responsibilities of headship—to love and protect his wife. God's incredibly awesome man, who was made in his own image, left his wife vulnerable and deceived, thus beginning the ultimate blame game.

I've often thought that, when I get to heaven, I'd like to share a few choice words with Adam. "You bum. Do you know what you did to me and the rest of mankind for these last thousands of years? The weeds, thorns, scorpions, snakes, stinging insects, vicious animals, disease, sweat, calamities, plagues, sexual sin, divorce, tears, heartache, murder, death, and a host of other curses are all your fault. You abdicated your responsibility. You did not protect your wife. You let her be seduced by the devil."

When Adam, the head of the human race, sinned and passed his sin down to the generations that followed, the greatest curse he could have passed on was the catastrophic result of his abdication of headship. And for the past many millennia, men have followed in his fallen footsteps. Let's be clear: the condition of sin was passed down through the generations from Adam's act of sin, not Eve's. Although Eve sinned first, it was not she but Adam who polluted the human race. It intuitively follows that only another man could rectify the results of that sin. Thus we have the grand and ultimate solution in the death of the last Adam, Jesus Christ. Adam's sin was rectified when Jesus died on the cross and presented to the Father his blood as the full and final payment for sin. Following that, it's our responsibility as believing men to rectify and reverse the sin of Adam by daily reclaiming our headship. We can no longer allow the world's greatest travesty, the abdication of headship, to wreak havoc in the lives of our wives and children—leaving them vulnerable to deception.

---

* The percentages noted in this section are from Sandy Kulkin and The Institute for Motivational Living (800-779-3472).

Men Are the Problem

If you don't think men are the problem, well then—that's a problem. Statistically men in this country account for the vast majority of alcoholics, drug addicts, felons, suicide victims, adulterers, rapists, and sex addicts. They are the most inclined toward anger, hostility, defensiveness, domestic violence, and desertions of their families. They are more prone to neglect responsibility and rely on others to take the blame. They find it difficult to admit wrong and rarely ask for forgiveness.

We watch the news, read the papers, and know what's going on in the workplace and next door. And, we know what goes on at home as well. Why has the male gender become the leader in all forms of sin? May I suggest that it all relates to the wholesale abdication by men of their headship responsibilities? God assigned husbands to be the heads; anything less than complete obedience and total compliance with his plan brings confusion and disorder to every part of a man's life. Keep in mind that as I address headship in this chapter, it is in the context of marriage only. Otherwise, the rules change, but even if some of us are not married, many of these principles still apply directly as guidance for how to honor and serve the women in our lives—from mothers, aunts, and sisters to work colleagues, neighbors, and the sweet little old ladies at church.

When Men Become Men

We have already discussed the amazing metamorphosis in men's personal lives when they understand how awesome they are in God. That same miraculous transformation occurs in their family life when they understand the principles of headship in marriage. When you embrace the fact that God called you to be the head in your marriage and family, you'll see real change. Imagine a new peace, direction, stability, wisdom, and security in the lives of your wife and children! Watch it

When the man is out of order, the woman is then out of order, the children will be out of order, society is out of order, and the church is out of order.

happen when you step up to the plate and assume your responsibilities of headship; the curse that Adam brought into the human race is reversed in practical ways on a daily basis.

Just as God made man to be awesome, he also made a husband to be the head of his wife. When a man assumes any other position than that of headship, he is "out of position" in his marriage and family. Not only has the forfeiture of headship kept men out of God's perfect will and blessing, it has positioned women in a place of responsibility they were never intended to occupy. This is why, in my opinion, Satan was able to seduce Eve in the first place. He approached her in a successful effort to circumvent Adam's headship. When the man is out of order, the woman is then out of order, the children will be out of order, society is out of order, and the church is out of order. Isn't that an exact description of our present society? But we need to change all that, one man at a time!

What the Bible Says

The Apostle Paul declares unequivocally in both Ephesians 1:22 and Colossians 1:18 that Jesus is the head of the church. In 1 Corinthians 11:3 he also says, "Now I want you to realize that the head of every man is Christ, and the head of the woman is man, and the head of Christ is God." In the great marriage chapter of Ephesians 5, Paul says it this way in verse 23: "For the husband is the head of the wife as Christ is the head of the church." If we want to understand what headship means, then all we need to do is look at how Jesus relates to the church. Jesus is the perfect example of how a man should treat his wife. However, before going into further detail on the definition of headship, it's important to establish its ubiquitous nature.

Everyone Is Under Headship

Have you considered that in God's kingdom everyone is under headship? The Greek word for *head* means "the source of direction and authority." It is applied to the Father, to Jesus, and to the husband. However, the wife is never biblically described as the head. Not that the woman can't be the head of a corporation, a business, a school, a department, or a government, but in marriage the man is defined as the head, and the woman is to submit to his headship. There can be many life areas over which a man is not responsible to be the head. But when it comes to marriage, God says he is the head.

Here's the headship hierarchy that Paul speaks of in 1 Corinthians 11:3:

- The FATHER
- The SON
- The Husband
- The Wife

Christ is under the headship of the Father, the man is under the headship of Christ, and the woman is under the headship of man.

Now, headship is not only a marriage issue. Everyone is under headship in some area. Every employee is under the headship of an employer. Every military man is under the headship of his superiors. Every child is under the headship of parents and school authorities. Every citizen is under the headship of civil authorities. Romans 13 makes clear that every person must submit to authority because all authority has been established by God. Consequently, to rebel against God's institution is the same as rebelling against God. If you believe as I do that mankind is not a result of evolution but rather creation, then it's imperative to understand headship. Then you'll better understand the creation process and mankind's earliest history. Look at some of these facts from the creation story found in Genesis 1-3 as well as Paul's emphasis found in Romans and 1 Corinthians.

- Man was made in the image of God. (Gen. 1:27; 1 Cor. 11:7)
- Woman was made from man, not man from woman. (Gen. 2:20-22; 1 Cor. 11:8)
- Man is the glory of God and woman is the glory of the man. (1 Cor. 11:7)

- Man's covering is Christ and a woman's covering is the man. (1 Cor. 11:3)
- Anatomically the woman was not made from the man's head but from his side and specifically identified by God as a suitable helper. (Gen. 2:20-22)
- Eve was deceived, but not Adam. (1 Tim. 2:14)
- Even though the woman sinned first, God first demanded accountability from the man for his actions. (Gen. 3:9-11)
- The result of Eve's sin was a singular judgment, pain in child-birth, passed down to every woman. Adam's sin, however, was corporate, infecting the entire human race with sin and death. (Gen. 3:17-24; Rom. 5:12,19; 8:20-21; 1 Cor. 15:21-22)

The Importance of Headship

It has always been interesting to me that the communion chapter in 1 Corinthians 11:17-34 is read at least monthly in most Christian churches. Yet, I've never heard one sermon on headship in relation to communion. Headship, the topic that is addressed in the first half of the chapter, forms the foundation for the later discussion of communion.

There is a reason why Paul mentions headship along with communion, and it must not be underestimated. The cross became necessary because the first man, Adam, the head of the human race, abdicated his headship responsibilities requiring the last Adam, Jesus, to re-establish headship through the cross. Paul tells us in Ephesians 1:9-10, "And he made known to us the mystery of his will according to his good pleasure, which he purposed in Christ, to be put into effect when the times will have reached their fulfillment—to bring all things in heaven and on earth together under one head, even Christ." Jesus has become, for we believing men, the picture of perfect headship, and we have the responsibility to follow his example.

Isaiah 1:5-6 makes it clear that when the head is sick, the entire body becomes diseased. Abdication of a husband's headship responsibilities brings death, confusion, and chaos to his marriage and family, polluting those whose lives his authority touches. Conversely, when a man exercises healthy headship in his marriage, it creates an environment of well-being, beginning with his wife and filtering down to his children, grandchildren, work associates, church fellowships, and everyone and everything else that he has influence in and over.

What is Headship?

The head of the natural body is the source of both direction and authority. The individual members of the physical body would be both powerless and directionless except for the head. The thumb, elbow, feet, eyes, and ears all provide needed functions for the body, but if not for the head, the body's individual functions would be random and confused. What brings all things together in purpose and function is the head. If the head, through injury or disease, is unable to produce the necessary direction, the body becomes dysfunctional and paralyzed.

Jesus is called the head of his body, the church, in Colossians 1. The head of the marriage provides the same function that Jesus provides for the church. If the man, the head of the marriage, fails to provide the necessary direction and authority in the marriage relationship, the entire body, the wife, children, and household will move into paralysis and atrophy.

I like to use the illustration of an umbrella to describe headship. An umbrella provides covering and direction for those who are standing underneath its protective canopy and choose to walk with the authority figure holding it. The most important thing a man can do is hold the umbrella. Many men, though, out of a misguided sense of their authority, feel it's their obligation to bark out orders, suppress the wife and children, make unilateral decisions, wield power without sensitivity, demand respect "because I said so," and in general be fairly obnoxious characters.

The biblical concept of headship which I'm describing here is to lead out of love, motivate through respect and appreciation, live a life that's exemplary, and serve to the point of sacrifice. In so doing, we honor God's will and wisdom, releasing our wives and families to be extensions of our authority which has been established and delegated to us under God's ultimate authority. In short, we hold the umbrella.

Through my submission to the headship of Jesus and the work of the Spirit, my wife and children will find in my headship an anchor of emotional stability. They will see consistency, trustworthiness, and dependability in my behavior and decisions. They will feel safe and, in real terms, they *will* be safe.

The Difference—Headship and Leadership

This brings us to a very important distinction.

If men are willing to grasp this, it will make a tremendous difference in our marriages and family lives. Most men think that headship and leadership are synonymous. *Wrong, Wrong, Wrong!* Headship in a marriage is a gender issue and leadership is a personality trait. You are the head of the marriage because you're the man, not necessarily because you're the best leader. Man is the head not because he is better than the woman, more intelligent, a better leader, the dominate personality, bigger and stronger, or the one who brings in the money. Man is the head only because God designed it this way. It is not a result of superiority but rather the result of design. Gentlemen, your wives are in no way inferior to you. God has simply designed you to occupy the role of headship. And, it is vitally important that you and all men understand that. You cannot function in effective headship unless you do!

On the other hand, *leadership* in the marriage *is* a personality issue. This is a crucial distinction that's difficult for some men to grasp but very necessary for real harmony in family life. In practical terms, marriage might consist of leadership combinations where the husband takes 60% of the leadership in the home and the wife 40%. Or it might be the reverse where a wife is the predominant leader. I personally think more women are natural leaders than men. Statistically, men with a strong leadership profile make up less than 5% of the male population. Which marriage partner accounts for the majority of leadership decisions in the home? Is it only obvious to me, because my wife is such a superior leader, that women might carry a big share of the leadership function? Is a woman's leadership potential in fact more common than men would like to admit?

Many men are often in the dark concerning the role and responsibilities of headship. They think that because men are the heads of the marriage they must also be the predominant leader in the home. Imagine what problems this thinking has created down through time! Men, you are scripturally obligated to be the heads of the marriage, but nothing in the Bible has required that you also be the predominating leaders. Remember, leadership is a personality trait, not a gender issue.

A man using good headship principles will know how to release the leadership potential of his spouse and still be comfortable in his own headship skin. His masculine pride and ego will not be threatened by her leadership gifts. Rather, he will find it a joy to turn her loose. Can you provide 20%, 30%, 40%, or 50% of the leadership percentage in the home and still be the head? Absolutely! You can't change your personality. God gave you your personality and wants you to keep it.

If you're a laid back personality, yet a man who works hard, brings home the paycheck, and loves your wife and kids, then so be it. That's great. If, by your personality, God has made you to be a 20% leader in the home, you don't have to feel guilty or condemned because you're not an 80% leader. Neither should you feel inferior to, or threatened by your wife, who might tip the leadership scales as an 80% leader in the home. You can totally relax in your headship, releasing your wife into her leadership.

Release Your Wife's Potential

If your wife is gifted in certain areas, release her to fulfill her leadership potential. That's called delegation. This is how you spread the authority of your headship to others. It will keep your authority from becoming unilateral and dangerous. Retain those areas of leadership you are more gifted in and release your wife to lead in those areas in which she is gifted. In this way, the two of you work together as one.

If your wife is gifted in certain areas, release her to fulfill her leadership potential.

Many men feel that if they release their spouses in their gift areas they might excel. Well, I hope so! To see your wife surpass you is the greatest compliment to your headship you could ever receive. Hopefully, everyone under your authority will be released to fulfill his or her leadership potential. Nothing brings me greater joy than to see my wife, Devi, as well as our children, Trina and Aaron, fully released into their leadership potentials. I am not threatened by their successes but rather truly honored and proud.

Many guys try to lead in areas where they aren't gifted. They won't let their wives take the lead. These fellas do it themselves and end up with a bad job! So, men—utilize your wives' talents.

One of my favorite sit-coms was *Home Improvement.* I could relate to virtually everything Tim Allen did on the show. He never asked for directions, rarely admitted mistakes, and always inadvertently punctured his own male ego balloon. Now, that's my kind of man! Pride is predominantly a male thing, and it's an Achilles heel for us! It's hard for a man to cry, to admit mistakes, to say he's sorry, or ever be seen as a failure. He's either right every time or he wants you to think he is.

I was walking out of a fast food restaurant one day and mistook a plate glass window for an open door. I hit it so hard I nearly broke my nose. The entire restaurant stopped talking and looked at me. But of course, being the man that I am, I couldn't admit I had just tried to walk into a plate glass window. I casually turned toward the crowd and waved to them as if to say, "I always walk into plate glass windows. It's no big deal." Then I went to the car and nearly cried from the pain. But my pride hurt far more than my nose. Men will do almost anything to avoid looking foolish or weak.

Give Direction to Your Wife

It is important to realize that all major direction will always start first with the head and then be distributed to the rest of the body. Every nerve ending, chemical release, muscle function, and motor coordination originates in the head. Jesus, the head of the church, receives direction from the Father and passes it on to the church. In the same way, the man is to receive direction from Jesus for his marriage and family and pass it on to the wife, his body.

This in no way means the man is the only one who can hear from God or that direction won't come occasionally from the wife and children. However, it does mean that God will never violate his headship principle and speak primarily to the wife or children first. My wife has often heard clearly from the Lord concerning details in our marriage and family, but primary direction for our future has always come to me first. Notice the words, "primary direction." A man would be foolish to think that God speaks only to him, but, conversely, he would also be foolish to think that God will speak to the various members of the family regarding primary direction prior to speaking to the head.

I've heard people facetiously say that God might speak first to the head, but the neck, meaning the wife, directs the head. That might solicit a laugh, but in real life, if the wife is continually giving direction to the husband, confusion always results in both the marriage and the family. On the other hand, any man taking a trip knows that failing to heed his wife's advice to stop and ask for directions is setting himself and his family up for a protracted trip with tension and frustration.

Men, none of us is perfect. We all make mistakes and we need to admit it when we do. But our mistakes, failures, inadequacies, and imperfections never change God's mind. He still speaks to the head and instructs the head to give direction to the body. When it's time to bring healing to a marriage, as is often the case, God will always start with the man. He will start with us. When God makes a man more emotionally and spiritually healthy, he brings health to that man's wife and family.

Your wife is naturally looking to your headship for stability. If you're insecure, she will be insecure. If you're fearful about the present or the future, she will feed into that fear. If you are wringing your hands and whining about the circumstances, she will suffer real insecurity and anxiety. The head provides covering, safety, clarity of vision, and strength of character. He is a pillar of faith. He is an anchor of stability for his family whether in a raging hurricane or in calm seas. Wives are happy to submit to this kind of headship. They'll take delight in the security and direction coming from their husbands.

Serving and Sacrificing

Men, this is so important! We must sacrificially serve our wives. This will keep headship from becoming dictatorial and suppressive. Not only have we been called to headship, but also we have been called to be the "Head Servant" in each of our households. Equality in marriage requires that we move from all the way up to all the way down—prayerfully and generously down to our knees. To love our wives as Christ loved the church is not only a good idea, it's a necessity. And the way we can love as Jesus did is to give ourselves sacrificially, to the point of death, for our wives. It is also accomplished through serving them first, providing for their needs ahead of our own. As we sacrifice, Paul says in Ephesians 5, we are treating our wives in the same way that Jesus treats the church.

I've yet to see a married couple come into my office for counseling that reflected a marriage built on selflessness, but I've counseled hundreds of couples who were consumed with selfish, "me-first" attitudes. The two of you, but especially you, should bust your "you-know-whats" attempting to out-serve the other. Make serving your spouse the priority of your life. Headship without "servantship" is dictatorship. And dictatorship will sink any ship, especially the ship of marriage.

Headship without "servantship" is dictatorship.

Though these same headship principles will work in any setting, they must first start in the marriage relationship. Serving, honoring, sacrificing, putting others first, preferring others before ourselves, earning respect through our selfless example, and unqualified love are actions and attitudes that will guarantee success. So men, I'm challenging you! Are you a man or a mouse? Squeak up!

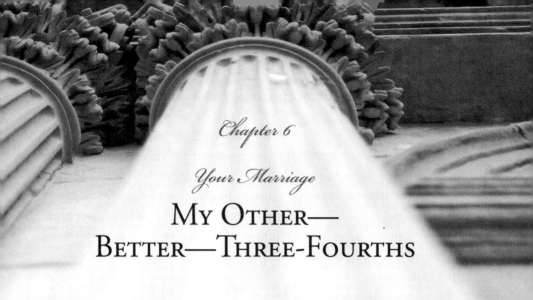

Chapter 6

Your Marriage

MY OTHER—
BETTER—THREE-FOURTHS

WHAT WORDS CAN I use to describe my wife? What image or picture could I use? A mere photo wouldn't do Devi justice. While it would reveal her outer beauty, it could not possibly demonstrate to you the depth and beauty of her character.

It was incredibly difficult for me to come up with a title for this chapter, a title which barely scratches the surface. How can I describe the greatest gift I have ever received next to Jesus? So, I think the best way for me to train men how to treat their wives is to use my own marriage as an example. My relationship with Devi is the best illustration of what I believe a man's marriage responsibility should be.

She is My Greatest Treasure

Devi is my pearl of great price. I value her more than anyone in the world. She brings heaven to earth. She continually builds me up. She adds class to everything I do. Solomon says the worth of such a wife is far above rubies, and he equates her with wisdom. (Solomon should know, since he had a lot of wives by any standard.) I'm grateful that the Holy Spirit speaks through Devi so often. His confirmations through her are as much of a blessing as when he speaks to me directly. It's not that I believe she is the Holy Spirit, but they sure sound alike at times. I cringe to think what it would be like without her voice and wisdom as God uses her to confirm his will to me.

Devi's voice is not negative. Rather, the tone she uses to share spiritual insight is the imploring speech of wisdom and patience, especially when I'm demanding my own way. She's the "prod" that makes me uncomfortable with the status quo and continually inspires me to improve. Without her motivational gifts (sometimes characterized best as the metaphoric "swift kick in the pants") from time to time, I might end up making the mistake of choosing to be content to remain in the nest of mediocrity until Jesus comes.

I was going to name this chapter "My Better Half." Yet, Devi is far more than just half of our marriage, and I have no doubt she thinks of me in the same way. Of course, I know when we were married God considered us two halves making a whole, but I'm just trying to find words to convey my sincere belief that she makes up more than half of our relationship.

In our marriage, I *literally* bring many things to the table. I love inviting people home for dinner. While I'm filling the glasses with ice and water, she has prepared a gourmet meal, set the table with our best china and silverware, torched the crème brûlée, folded the napkins, put on the background music, and lit the candles—all while entertaining the guests. Meanwhile, I'm still filling the water glasses. As I say, she's more than half our marriage!

When it's time to make a significant decision around the home, I begin the process with a few shallow thoughts like, "How much does it cost?" or "How much work will it take?" or "How does it affect me?" Meanwhile, Devi dives in headfirst and begins methodically delineating goals, costs, timeframes, organizational strategy, graphs of all pertinent variables, labor needed, and projected results. She has immediate suggestions for a course of action while it can take me days to process the basic information, the key implications, and the potential pros and cons of any decision.

Devi also really knows how to communicate in both large crowds and small groups. She's articulate, clear, concise, sensitive, and personable. I, on the other hand, can talk in circles, beat around the bush, seldom come to a clear conclusion, don't necessarily say what I mean, and sometimes leave listeners in a state of confusion. It's great for me that Devi can come along behind, sweep up the mess, and clarify what I really meant to say. Bless her. She's definitely three-fourths of our relationship.

The World's Greatest Woman

I met Devi when she was only—gulp—thirteen, and I was seventeen. I was a freshman in college, and she was a freshman in high school. Even then, she was more mature than I was. Actually, I've just started catching up to her maturity these past few years. Or was it this year? At any rate, she was four years and four months my junior. Being the spiritual leader that I am, I waited until she was sixteen to propose to her. I didn't want anyone to say, "What were you thinking? Were you trying to obey the scriptural admonition to train up a child in the way she should go?" Then, two weeks after her seventeenth birthday in Salinas, California, we both said, "I do!" And we've been "we-doing" ever since. This year, we celebrated our forty-sixth (or was it our forty-seventh?) anniversary. Well, you know how it is; they change every year, so it's hard to keep track.

At the time of our marriage, I was a District Youth Director for a denomination in the Northwest. I remember asking her one day, "Honey, when I ask for all the teenagers to stand up in the congregation, do you mind *not* standing up?"

Those were the good old days when we didn't have enough money to buy two hamburgers, so we'd buy one and split it. We were traveling all over the Northwest preaching in small towns. We were put up in some terrible overnight accommodations that many times were without clean sheets or inside toilets. I'm telling you, it stunk...literally.

At one of these "accommodations," the pastor had converted an old one-room school house into a church. He lived in the back with his family and put us in the attic above the front entrance. It was necessary to climb a ladder to our guest room, giving new meaning to the words "Upper Room." Then we had to stand on the bed and pull a string to turn on the light. After dressing for bed, we pulled down the covers only to find dirty sheets. Fortunately, Devi was as wise then as she is today. We'd had an experience or two with dirty sheets in our early travels. Unbeknownst to our pastor host, she pulled out a clean pair of sheets and changed the bed. Then we stood on the bed again, pulled the string and tried to get some sleep. If we happened to be leaving the next morning, she would return the bed to its original dirty status to await the next blessed guest.

On this particular occasion, she was sick and had to get up several times during the night. Up on the bedsprings she would stand, trying to balance long enough to find the string and pull it. She would then put on her robe, pad through the church sanctuary in the dark, go into the pastor's quarters in the rear of the building, and use the toilet. Of course, the toilet hadn't yet been plumbed, so she would have to draw a bucket of water and fill the toilet. Then back through the church she would pad and return to bed after first ascending the ladder, standing on the bed, waking me up again—which I tolerated with incredible grace—and pulling the string. And this happened four times that night! Those were the good old days? What am I saying? The "good old days" weren't really so good. I'd really rather not go back to them.

I don't know when it happened that I started to understand the blessing I'd received, but it was not nearly soon enough. Slowly at first, it began to dawn on me what an incredible wife I had. She never, and I mean *never*, complained. Instead, everywhere we went she would train young women in homemaking, communication, and life-skills. She was already developing the concepts she would eventually use in her *Mentoring Mansion Intensives for Women* on the "Use What You Have" principle. I hope the light will turn on for you gentlemen much sooner than it did for me. I can't tell you the day, month, or year when it happened, but there came a time when I was acutely aware of God's greatest gift to me next to his Son.

Along with the revelation of my "greatest treasure" came a tremendous sense of responsibility to begin responding to my wife like Jesus did to the church. How do I value, honor, and respect her? How do I express love and appreciation to her? How do I treat her in front of others? How do

I emotionally and physically love her in front of our children? How do I serve her? How does she feel after being in my presence?

I had incredible respect for the late President Ronald Reagan. My appreciation for the President had nothing to do with his foreign or domestic policies, or even his leadership in bringing down the despised Berlin Wall.

My esteem for the President was based on the way he treated his wife, Nancy. On one occasion he confided to his Vice-President, "She's the only woman I know who I can get homesick for as soon as she walks out of the room." And did you notice how he treated her in public? He treated her like a diamond tiara carried on a pillow.

On the other hand, nothing makes me as sick as seeing a man berate his wife in public. It's bad enough for him to degrade her privately, but it's inexcusable when it's done in public. I don't even like to see a man walking ahead of his wife.

Men, you need to carry your wife's picture in your wallet. Then you can continually dig into your back pocket and remind yourself of the greatest treasure you have on this earth. It would be a tragic mistake for you to give all your attention and affection to your children, your work, or others only to neglect your spousal pearl of great price—your help-meet jewel of inestimable value. I cannot go through a day without telling Devi many times how much I love her. I can just look at her and praise God for my gift.

When we're apart, having been called on to speak at different venues, I will often, in prayer or in a phone call to her, speak words of praise and voice the tremendous gratitude I have for Devi. I also make it a point to introduce my messages with comments of praise and admiration for her.

A Teleios Man Loves His Wife as Christ Loves the Church

The apostle Paul commands men to love their wives as Christ loved the church (Ephesians 5:22-23). Men, listen up on this! It is not your wives but *you* who are commanded to be the lovers. Very clearly, the Bible places the obligation to be a spiritual, marital lover squarely on men— another opportunity to express headship and servantship.

The most important biblical definition of *love* is found in the Greek word *agape*. It is always an action word. Something must be *done*. We must *show* our love for our wives through our actions. It can mean everything from spoken words, to an embrace, to flowers, to building her up publicly, to listening to her, to taking out the garbage, to opening her car door, to writing love notes, to taking her to special places. But first and foremost it means *to serve her*. Don't say you love your wife unless you prove it with your actions. Words without actions are devoid of love; they are empty and meaningless. And please don't dare attempt a close encounter of the intimate kind unless love is the driving motivation. Sex without love is both damaging and demeaning.

Make Her Holy with Your Words

Paul calls upon the husband to love his wife as Christ loves the church—which is obviously to the point of death. He commands the man to make her holy by "the washing with water through the word." Although it's not obvious in the English text, this verse in Ephesians 5:26 uses the word, *rema* for *word* rather than the usual *logos*. Understanding this will help you in the interpretation.

Paul is not saying you should be continually quoting scripture (logos) to your spouse. He is saying that you are to speak cleansing, encouraging, honoring, affirming, and edifying words (rema) to her. It's your words, not God's Word, which Paul is referring to in this verse. Your words have the power to bring out the best or the worst in your wife.

In the same book of Ephesians, in the fourth chapter, verse 29, Paul says, "Do not let any unwholesome talk come out of your mouths, but only what is helpful for building others up..."

You are to speak only those words which build her up.

I was riding along in a truck with a friend one day, and he got a call on his cell phone. After he hung up I asked him, "Who were you were talking to?"

"My wife," he responded.

"Do you always talk to your wife like that?" I asked.

Ouch! He immediately knew what I was talking about. The words we use when speaking to our greatest treasure should be our most edifying, encouraging, and affirming words!

You should speak in the same way to your children. If your own wife and children don't respect you, it won't matter if anyone else does. They will only honor you if you first honor them by your words and actions. After all, how can the world's most awesome man have married anyone less than the world's most incredible woman and together have produced the world's most incredible children? Because they *are* incredible, edify them and speak life into them with all kinds of encouraging words.

The word for "unwholesome" in the NIV translation of Ephesians 4:29 is the Greek word *sapros*. It refers to anything that devalues something. Your words either cause your wife to feel valued or devalued. If something you say makes your wife feel devalued, demeaned, denigrated, defamed, or diminished in her own eyes or those of others, you have failed in your obligation to verbally lift her up.

I think we need to establish this truth with a verbal commitment of acceptance. In the form of a prayer it would sound like this: *Jesus, in your name I commit my tongue to speak only words of affirmation and encouragement to my wife. I will not say anything that reduces her sense of value. I will speak only those words that edify and build her up.*

Guys, go ahead and commit this promise to the Lord and to your wife. Say it out loud so that every word can become a commitment. Paul says that your words have the cleansing power to make her holy. What husband wouldn't want that?

Making Our Wives Glorious

The final instruction of Paul to husbands in Ephesians 5:27 is to make your wife glorious. The Greek word for "glorious" or as the NIV translates it, "radiant," is *endoxis* which can be translated variously as:

- Honored
- Esteemed
- Renowned

- Magnificent
- Extraordinary

Can you imagine what could happen in your life if your wife was honored, esteemed, renowned, and magnified? That's the goal of Jesus for you. Jesus wants *you* to be his greatest expression on this earth. Shouldn't your wife be *your* greatest expression on the earth?

My joy in life is to see my wife become outstanding. I will do anything in my power to make sure that happens. Because of her outstanding ministry to women, my wife is well on her way to national acclaim. I can hardly wait to put the tiara on her head and proclaim, "You are as beautiful as the Bride of Christ." By the time Jesus returns or I pass into eternity, I want my wife to be as beautiful, cleansed, radiant, and perfect as the Bride of Christ. I have the God-given ability to make her that way. Your wife is your own body, because in Christ you have become one. So, while you are elevating your wife to a place of supreme importance under Christ, you are elevating yourself as well. That should be a reason to shout, "Hallelujah!"

Love is a Choice

I received a call recently from a young man who says he no longer loves his wife. He fell in love with another woman.

Of course, I have a problem with that. "Falling in love" and "falling out of love" is based on a worldly Hollywood definition of love. Biblical love is not based on the fleeting and temporary infatuations expressed in pop music and romance novels.

Biblical love is not an emotion that we fall in or out of. No, it's a *choice* we make to give ourselves sacrificially to another. As soon as love becomes a selfish act, it no longer qualifies as love. We don't "fall out of love." A man makes a conscious decision if he chooses to stop loving his wife because she is either doing something that displeases him or else isn't doing something that pleases him. Admit it. It's a totally selfish choice you make to stop loving based on how she is or is not treating you. More than that, it's really just a cop-out or rationalization. Rather than dealing with the issues, you take the easy way out and start "falling in love" with someone else. Well, I've got news for you. If you haven't yet learned how to choose to love, the next marriage won't work either.

Love is a choice. I choose to love my wife. I choose to love her every day. I've been making the same choice for the past forty-six years. My choice to love extends to other people as well. I choose to love people; not because of what they do for me, but because of what God did for me through his Son, Jesus. God has commanded me to love them, and God has commanded me to love my wife. When I choose to love my wife, God honors me with blessings that are uncontainable.

Before I was married, my future father-in-law gave me some sage advice. I just knew it was too simplistic. He said that I should never go to sleep without first kissing my wife. *How silly*, I thought. *He must not know there will never be a time when I won't kiss my wife goodnight before going to sleep.* But three months later I found out he was right to share that simple but significant principle with me. I distinctly remember lying in bed thinking, *If she thinks I'm going to kiss her goodnight, she's wrong. She displeased me today, so no kiss for her. She's just not going to be blessed tonight. Tough luck, baby.*

While I was lying there, I thought of my father-in-law's instruction. So I decided to give her a little peck on the cheek. That felt so good I decided then to give her a little smooch. Then it turned into a full-blown kiss on the lips. By the time I finished this three course meal, I had forgotten completely what I was mad about. The next day I realized that what had made me mad wasn't anything she'd done. It was something dumb I had done. I just didn't want to admit it. If I hadn't made the choice to be obedient to love, I would have missed out on an important early lesson on how choices affect a person. If love was something a person just "falls out of," I could have "fallen out" within three months of "falling in."

Love is a decision, not an emotion. Say it out loud, "Love is a decision, not an emotion!" If you run your love on emotions, you're going to go bankrupt.

I love the illustration that Bill Bright gave at a seminar that I attended years ago in Oakland, California. He said emotions are

If you run your love on emotions, you're going to go bankrupt

like the caboose on a train. The engine symbolizes the fact of the Word of God, the coal car is the belief in the fact, and the emotions are the caboose. Emotions are good as a caboose but make a terrible engine. If emotions run the engine, your train will run in reverse. It doesn't take long to realize how devastating things can become if you allow emotions to determine your future.

Strive for Unity

God wants unity. The Father, Son, and Spirit are all in unity. Jesus's prayer in Gethsemane in John 17:21 was that his disciples would be in unity as were he and the Father. The reason Jesus gave the five-fold office gifts of apostle, prophet, pastor, teacher, and evangelist to the church was "to prepare God's people for works of service" and to see the church come into unity (Eph. 4:12). In Ephesians 4:3, Paul says we are to make every effort to keep the unity of the spirit through the bond of peace. He goes on to say, "…there is one body, and one Spirit—just as you were called to one hope when you were called—one Lord, one faith, one baptism; one God and Father of all, who is over all and through all and in all" (Eph. 4:4-6).

God wants a husband and wife to be unified as well. Read Matthew 19:5 where Jesus quoted Genesis 2:23. Look also at Mark 10:7-8, 1 Corinthians 6:16 and Ephesians 5:31. God makes it clear that he wants the husband and wife to leave family and home and cleave to each other until the two become one. Unity is the process of becoming one. In the process of unity, a couple becomes not one in person, but one in *purpose*.

If there is an over-arching prayer I have for you and your wife, it is for the two of you to become one. Couples can live together for years and still not be one. What a tragedy! They can be married fifty years and still not be unified. And just because couples are Christians doesn't necessarily mean they are one. The two must *become* one and, contrary to popular opinion, it has nothing to do with compatibility. It has everything to do with their willingness and choice (there's that word again) to comply with God's laws of unity.

How Does Unity Happen in Marriage?

Recognize Headship. As discussed in the last chapter, there must be a clear recognition of headship. In every case, headship always precedes unity, whether it is in a marriage, church, government or job. Who is the head of the marriage? We have established that the man is the head according to the Bible.

The Head Must Establish Equality. As soon as headship is identified, the head must establish equality. As I will teach throughout this book, unless the head of the marriage takes upon himself the form of a servant, equality will never be realized. If the man doesn't begin serving his wife and family, he will remain a dictator. His authority will be established through control and thus disqualify him from being a godly leader.

Physically mirror unity. There are many physical things you can do as a couple to nurture a pattern of unity in your lives. I encourage you to make an effort to practice each of these activities in your marriage.

Walk with her. It sounds so simplistic, but you'd be surprised how many couples don't walk together.

Hold her hand. This also sounds simplistic, like something you'd only do when dating. Nonsense! Everywhere you go, you need to hold hands.

Sit by her at social events as well as at home.

Touch her affectionately as often as possible.

Kiss her every chance you get. Bedtime kisses are great but shallow if that's the only time you kiss.

Work together. Plan projects where you can be together, each contributing what he or she does best.

Sleep together. While this may sound silly to some, many married couples, for whatever reason, do not sleep together. If there is a valid reason why you don't sleep together, at least begin or end the night together. Nothing can replace the marriage bed for intimacy.

Value each other's input. Don't make major decisions without talking them over as husband and wife. Whether the decision is right or wrong is less important than whether you make it together.

Consider your spouse to be more important than yourself. Because selfishness is the major reason for division in a marriage, the only way to break it and force it out of your marriage is to put your wife's interests ahead of your own.

Stop arguing for your point! You've heard both men and women say, "But if I let them think they're right, they'll think they've won—I can't do that!" We're not in an army and trying to win the war of right and wrong. You are meant to be one with your spouse. If one of you loses, you both lose. If one of you wins, you both win. We should be striving for win-win, not win-lose outcomes. Win-lose outcomes are really just lose—lose outcomes.

Let love be the foundation and motivation of all you do. Read Paul's definition of love in 1 Corinthians 13 and ask yourself how you measure up to the standard. Meeting the standard is not only possible, it must be met if you wish to establish unity in your marriage. By the way, you begin with patience, and you can start working on that today.

Forgive each other as soon as there is an offense. Forgiveness must be immediate and complete. Don't let the sun go down on you wrath (Eph. 4:26). Apologize immediately for things you have said or done wrong. Don't qualify your apology with, "I did this because you did that." If you do, it won't count as an apology. Furthermore, don't hold grudges. They will kill you. Jesus said in Matthew 6:15 that if you don't forgive others when they sin against you, your Father in heaven can't forgive you when you sin.

> *Pray for your spouse the same way Jesus prayed for you, that you would become one. If you have been living as two people rather than one, God doesn't want you living that way any longer. He wants you to be united in purpose, thought, and action, just as Jesus is with his Bride.*

Divorce is Out of the Question

Lastly, I want to tell you what I believe about divorce. Before I do, however, I want to be clear that for all of you who have been affected in some way by divorce, I am absolutely not pointing a finger of condemnation your way. I believe in and teach the grace of God in these situations. So, I'm not addressing what has happened in the past but what our view of the future must be according to God's Word. That said, the best description of my feelings on divorce is found in Malachi 2:16, "'I hate divorce,' says the LORD God of Israel." Ditto, Ditto, Ditto! My feelings, precisely!

Jesus expressed the same disdain for divorce in Matthew 19:6 when he said, "Therefore what God has joined together, let man not separate."

Some Pharisees had come to Jesus to test him on the subject of divorce "for any and every reason." They argued Moses had given them the OK as long as the man gave his wife a "certificate of divorce." Jesus responded, "Moses permitted you to divorce your wives because your hearts were hard. But it was not this way from the beginning."

Addressing issues of divorce, whether it relates to you or someone you know, is futile. I cannot possibly know the reasons that brought you or your friends to make this difficult decision. Our lives are under the blood of Jesus and we appeal to the grace of God in these matters. However, I can say unequivocally that God is opposed to divorce. And because God is resolutely against anything that would break the marriage contract, it is imperative that we have the same attitude.

Hate is a strong word. But God uses that word when referring to divorce. God is for marriage and keeping the marriage vows inviolate. He opposes anything that would come against marriage. Therefore, we must also hate divorce. For you married men and remarried men, beginning today, never ever bring up the word *divorce* in your vocabulary. Don't even think about it. Don't discuss it with your wife or children. Put it out of your mind. Make a decision today that regardless of how tough things get, you will never resort to divorce. You love God too much, fear his Word too much, love your wife too much, and love your kids too much to ever consider divorce.

Make a decision today that regardless of how tough things get you will never resort to divorce.

Billy Graham's wife says that divorce has never been an option, but she has considered murder. Obviously neither action is an option. What makes her statement attractive is that she'd already excluded divorce as a possibility. How many marriages dangerously close to the precipice of divorce have, by the grace of God and the will of both parties to make the tough choices, rebounded to be stronger than ever? How many marriages and families have been saved through God's grace and parents' courageous choices? God is a God who doesn't give up or tire and neither should we.

Perhaps Winston Churchill's famous comments uttered in a grade school during the dark days of World War II should sum up your own opinion on divorce: "We will never, never, never, never, never give up!" Amen! You need that bull-dog approach to marriage. Make a declaration! Regardless of what happens you will never give up, you will never stop praying, you will never forsake your vows, and you will never retreat or be unfaithful to your wife. Determine once and for all that you will never, never, never, never, never give up!

Now go out right now and give your wife a hug and kiss!

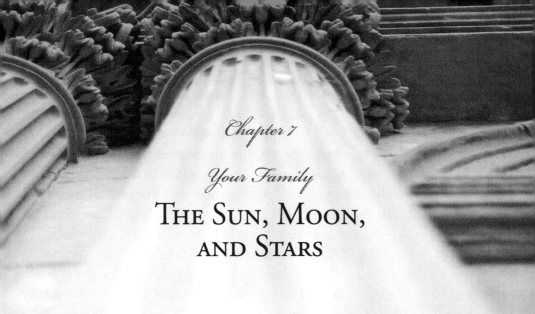

Chapter 7

Your Family

THE SUN, MOON, AND STARS

I'M WRITING THIS CHAPTER on Christmas Day at the home of my daughter, Trina, in Colleyville, Texas. On the table in front of me sits a picture of Trina and her husband, James. The picture frame is inscribed, "And He took the children in His arms and blessed them" (Mark 10:16). My mother-in-law, who has joined us for Christmas this year at Trina's home, will soon be moving here, as her husband passed away in October. And no, I don't have any mother-in-law jokes to tell. She's an absolutely incredible woman. We're family.

A few days earlier, I was at our home in Youngstown, Ohio, and had an early Christmas with my son, Aaron, and his family from Jamestown, North Carolina. We get to see my son only a few times a year, but it's like Christmas every time we get together. It's because we're family.

On the Monday before, I was in the Pennsylvania State Correctional Institution at Rockview visiting Gene McGuire, AK4192. Gene is in prison for life. I have visited him every birthday, Thanksgiving, Christmas, and almost monthly, for the past twenty years. In addition to our visits with Gene, we see Rafael, Jim, Scott, and Orlando. We celebrate the holidays with them as well. They're part of our family too.

Over the years, Devi and I have had over eighty young people live in our home. Scores of people have been born again there in our home. We've tried to make Jesus easy to find within our four walls. Then, of course, during my travels, I have the habit of adopting anyone I see in need of a spiritual dad. So that adds several hundred more to our family unit. It's hard to think of a Christmas or Thanksgiving where we haven't added plates to the table. Those bonding strings of a family table are powerful and nurturing. Well, guess what? My kids have followed suit, and every holiday they bring in the strays and lonely hearts.

On one particular Thanksgiving, my son and daughter-in-law, Kim, invited us to their home in Greensboro, North Carolina. It's nice to have grown kids who can reciprocate, right? Aaron and Kim also decided to invite a deeply troubled, dysfunctional woman to have dinner with us. To say she was strange would be an understatement. Throughout the day I kept thinking, *Why did Aaron and Kim invite this woman? Why can't we just have Thanksgiving with our family alone for once?* And then it occurred to me: this is how we trained them. This *is* our family, which includes the solitary and unlovely, the rejected and deeply troubled. We want everyone to experience the family environment.

What would we do if we weren't family? God never intended for us to live single, detached, or separated lives. "Even the solitary he places in families" (Ps. 68:6). He wants us to be joined at the heart. He wants us to co-exist as a family unit. Even God exists in the "family" of Father, Son, and Holy Spirit—mutually bound to each other in love. Make no mistake about it: God is in the family-making business.

God never intended for us to live single, detached, or separated lives.

We live in a culture that values independence, and yet gets further and further away from the hearth and heart of home. We are deep down, however, a people who yearn to belong and connect. The heart still cries for relationships which transcend the fleeting, ephemeral commitments of this age. People still want to have a place to go—a place they can call home. Indeed, people are desperately seeking a place where people will love them and they can love people. Our hearts respond to the tugging from the loving gravity of a family.

The family is the bedrock and foundation of all relationships. As more and more families are being alienated by divorce, those caught up in the destruction must eventually find people and places to satisfy their deep cry for relationships. But these folks seldom find such places and people. This is the great and growing dilemma of our time.

In the final chapter of the Old Testament, Malachi prophesied that God will send Elijah in the last days to turn the hearts of the fathers to the children and the children to the fathers. Perhaps this is the generation, before the coming of the Lord, when hearts will once again turn toward home. Maybe, just maybe, you and I can change the course of our culture by insisting on the priorities of family and home. Quite possibly you can be that husband and father who refuses to buy into the devil's lie that the home is just a place to hang your hat.

The Galactic Family

In Genesis 37, Joseph describes a dream to his family. He saw the sun, moon, and stars bowing down to him. This dream was a preview from God. One day in his future, Joseph would be able to save his family from starvation. This story speaks about a specific situation at a certain moment in history. But look closely. This cosmic vision of the sun, moon, and stars allows us to catch a glimpse of God's design for all families. God's paradigm is that the home be led by the father, followed by the mother, and ringed by the children. Although this has been the principal pattern for millennia, today's thinking seems bent on contradicting this pattern, as if a new method might be an improvement on God's original design.

Today there are multiple marriages and divorces. Unmarried couples live together; homosexual couples "marry" and adopt. Single parents struggle to raise children, and children sue and even "divorce" themselves from their parents. Moms work and stay-at-home dads try to be the mom. We have gone down a path of dysfunctional family life in the last five decades. It might be more correct to characterize it all as family *existence* rather than family life. It's as if the solar system is askew with planets spinning off in all directions. Dad is no longer the sun, the father of the children and head of the wife. Mom is no longer the moon, a reflection of her husband, the sun. She is either attempting by choice or is forced by circumstances to be the center of the solar system. With the homosexual agenda, we have either two suns in the family or two moons, depending on your viewpoint. And the stars, created to bring honor to their parents, now oppose them and seek to take over the entire solar system.

Planets and galactic bodies now collide. Enter Hollywood to take advantage of the drama, just as they continue to make substantial contributions to this chaotic picture. Movies turn this monumental tragedy into humor, so we can all laugh along as the family is being systematically destroyed.

When was the last time you saw a movie in which the father wasn't portrayed as a bumbling idiot, the mother wasn't dominant, the children weren't disrespectful, or the family wasn't dysfunctional?

Kids are in greater and greater control of the entire solar system, check with any school teacher or counselor.

Things are definitely in a state of confusion. Our family solar system is warped and out of balance. It's no wonder that Malachi calls out to the human race to bring the fathers back to their families and the children to their fathers as we await Messiah's return.

Components of a Healthy Family

Parents are often conflicted and overwhelmed with the issues they face today. It's understandable that we might simply stick our heads in the sand. There are huge cultural pressures on marriages, and, sometimes the rules of the road are confusing and unclear.

God has provided a very specific roadmap to which we can turn, and the Holy Spirit has been called alongside to give us direction. With that in mind, the following are a few thoughts on the makeup of a healthy family.

Men, you can tell I like lists; they are succinct and provoke action. So here is a list of family "to do's" based on the principles of God's Word.

- Your family has priority over your work, church activity, personal recreation, and other activities or interests. When you allow a pervasive and imbalanced pattern of scheduled or unscheduled activity to invade your family life, insidious decay starts. Such intrusions automatically erode the foundations of stability and unity in the home. Don't let extracurricular activities interrupt your home life. Your home life should determine your activities.

- Show your children your love, sensitivity, and respect for their mother. Hug her often in front of your children. Model how a man should love his wife.

- Maintain an atmosphere of peace in the home. Shouting, screaming, accusing, and arguing should all be totally banned. The words, "Shut up!" should especially be off-limits. Watch out for atmosphere-destroyers such as loud or confusing music, arguing or fighting among the children, or intrusive television noise, in fact, distracting noise of any kind.

- Allow children to be part of the adult world. Have them participate in adult conversations and learn to wait their turn. Also, take them with you on trips, errands, and runs to the grocery store. They need to feel they're part of your life and you are part of theirs. *Talk respectfully to your children, and you will earn their respect.*

- Every member of the family should take on responsibilities and tasks in the home—no exceptions. It's unhealthy for either the mother or the father to do all the work. Everyone should help carry the load. Everyone should work.

- In some way, involve your family with mission projects or trips, feeding the poor, and world evangelism. Teach them how to give not only their money, but themselves as well.

- Be involved in your children's ministry, school, and sports activities.

- Take vacations. Children seldom remember what you purchased *for* them but they will never forget what you did *with* them.

- Husbands, encourage your wives to be involved in some of your activities and commit to be involved in some of hers. She may say, "Well, I don't like football," and show little interest in watching it with you. Encourage her to join you, even if only for a few minutes, as an opportunity to just sit together. Make sure you show her some attention while she's sitting with you. For your part, go shopping with your wife once in a while. Most men don't enjoy shopping, but we need to simply "be" with our wives. Sometimes they like that! Unless you participate in each other's activities, you'll drift apart. You must take advantage of every opportunity to bond closer together.

- Eat together. My wife, Devi, was searching for core reasons explaining the dissolution of the American family. She felt the Lord saying, "Families have left the dinner table." Yes, we have stopped eating together. The family today is always on the run, eating out, and grabbing meals at fast food restaurants. We eat in the car and in front of the television. We eat at home but at separate times. Eating together develops family cohesion, unity, and health and develops social graces and emotional maturity in our children.

- Help your wife at every opportunity. Find excuses to serve her. Take the load off her as much as possible. Men, we have little concept of how tiring it can be for a wife who spends all her time with children.

- Don't allow sibling rivalry. It tears down the unity of the family. My daughter claims this to be the single reason why her children are so tightly knit together. She says it is because she would not allow fighting among them.

- Be consistent in everything from your prayer and Bible reading habits to how you discipline the children. Consistency will produce security in your children and peace in the family.

I'm going to close this section with some thoughts from John and Linda Friel. In their book of the same title, these authors have listed the following "seven worst things parents do:"

1. Baby a child.
2. Put a marriage last.
3. Push a child into too many activities.
4. Ignore their own spiritual and emotional lives.
5. Try to be their child's "best friend."
6. Fail to give their child structure.
7. Expect a child to fulfill the parents' personal dreams.[*]

All I can say to that, John and Linda, is, "Amen! Amen! Amen!"

Raising Winning Children

I know of no better guide for a parent to use in training children than Psalm 23. It provides the perfect outline for raising *winning, godly* children. In the same way the Lord was the Good Shepherd shaping David's

---

[*] Friel, *The 7 Worst Things Parents Do*, chapter titles.

life, so should parents be deeply involved in shaping the lives of their children. There are several major objectives we should be seeking in raising our children.

First and most importantly, we want our children to experience a personal relationship with God. This is not something you can accomplish for them, but you can certainly share with them the message of God's love and pray for the work of the Holy Spirit in their lives.

In addition, our children must develop godly character and live by biblical principles. In so doing, they will become all God intended them to be, living responsible lives—people who are generous, compassionate, and sensitive to others.

Throughout the training process of raising winning children, see yourself as the steward, not the owner, of their lives. Biblically, God possesses everything. We are only the stewards of his possessions, working on his behalf.

Good Parenting According to Psalm 23

In Psalm 23, the Shepherd demonstrates four major tasks necessary to positively mold a child's character: "The Lord is my shepherd, I shall not want. He *makes* me lie down in green pastures; He *leads* me beside quiet waters. He *restores* my soul; He *guides* me in the paths of righteousness for His name's sake" (NASB, emphasis added). Let's analyze this process by process:

The Discipline Process: The good parent "makes" the child.

As a child grows in understanding and reasoning, we must establish discipline in the child's life, teaching them the *absolutes* in life. These are found in the Word of God, embodied in the Ten Commandments as detailed in Exodus 20. Some of God's absolutes include *honesty* at all times and regardless of circumstance, the *worship of God alone,* and the truth that *stealing is always wrong* and must be repented of with restitution. We teach the truth that all forms of *sexual activity* outside of heterosexual marriage are wrong. Another primary truth is that *authority* must be respected.

It is imperative as a parent that you establish clear guidelines and expectations. For example, you might disallow any form of disrespect or "talking-back" or "sassing." A defiant "no" should never be tolerated. This teaches them to respect parental authority. They must also learn to respect all other forms of authority. In so doing, they will learn the principles of submission. Instruct them about what they can and cannot do and let them know the consequences of breaking the rules. Be sure to follow through on the consequences. This will teach them the necessity and benefit of setting boundaries in their lives.

Let your children know that temper tantrums in all forms will not be tolerated. This will teach them self-control. Never allow them to raise their voice to you. Any questions or comments should be spoken at a normal voice level. This will teach them control of attitudes.

Convey to them your expectation of the same behavior when they are away from you as when they are with you. This teaches them self-discipline. Finally, teach them to keep their word. This will teach them the foundation of all character.

I recognize our current culture frowns upon corporal punishment. Yet, the Bible could not be clearer. God instructs parents to spank children in such passages as Proverbs 13:24, 22:15, 23:13-14, and 29:15. Because he does, it's important to establish guidelines consistent with the Word of God.

First, only use spanking as a form of punishment when the misbehavior is a direct act of rebellion. Spanking should never be a reactionary hit or a "slap on the wrist" but a deliberate and thorough action strong enough to be remembered as a firm consequence for disobedience. Spanking should be applied to the part of the anatomy that has the natural padding—the bottom-side.

Secondly, physical discipline should always be controlled and *never administered in anger*. Spanking is an act of love and love cannot be administered in a fit of rage. Beatings are not scriptural and are counterproductive, often producing rebellion rather than the positive outcome for which a spanking is intended.

Finally, after the punishment, the child should be hugged, affirmed, and told they are loved. *Do not tell the child what they did wrong, but have them tell you what they did wrong.* This way they will learn to admit failures. Also, the child will understand the reason for the spanking and not feel accused. For every act of disobedience there should be a corresponding consequence commensurate in severity with the weight of the infraction. Don't discipline more severely than the violation demands. The ultimate goal of discipline is to bring your child to the place where he/she will experience the rewards of living a disciplined life.

The Modeling Process: The good parent leads the child.

Fathers, this is *so* important! We *must* demonstrate any behavior that we demand. Hypocrisy confuses a child. Our words will carry little lasting weight with our kids if we don't practice what we preach. And we know for sure that they're watching. As in every other area of life, our actions speak louder than words to our children.

The following suggestions should go without saying, but I'm going to say them anyway. First of all, we model a love for God by making him the first priority in our lives. Be the same person in the home as you are at church. Be consistent. Again, be the first to do whatever you expect from your child. Pray and read your Bible openly before your children, so they can pattern their lives after you. Love their mother lavishly, particularly in their presence. Demonstrate a life of gratefulness so your children won't grow up with demanding or presumptuous attitudes. Be quick to apologize when you are wrong so they can witness your humility before God and the family. Finally, model a servant's heart, demonstrating to your family the values of serving and sharing.

The Affirmation Process: The good parent restores the child.

We might say that establishing discipline in the life of your children is only one side of the parenting equation. Another term in this side of the equation is the affirmation of your child. The math is simple: Discipline + Affirmation = Confidence.

My heart breaks as I think of this. Nothing is more important in the lives of our kids than receiving constant affirmation from their fathers. This is a powerful weapon in our fight against generational dysfunction. This "building up" process assures our children have confidence as they face life's pressures and challenges. Yet, many fathers don't affirm their kids. Later in their lives, these children look everywhere for affirmation. Men, affirm your kids now, and keep them off wrong paths in their futures!

Edify and compliment your children in front of others and correct them privately. Don't threaten them or use fear tactics as a method of training. Take them with you and keep them near you as much as possible. Say, "I love you" and touch them often—hugs, kisses, and love pats are essential to emotional stability. Don't call them negative names, i.e., "stupid," "dumb," "clumsy," or "fat." Don't compare them with other children. Always respect them and honor their individuality. After they complete a project, don't tell them how you would have done it differently or better.

Don't allow yourself to be threatened if they take differing viewpoints as they grow older. Let them express different opinions without characterizing them as rebellious. As they mature enough to understand, explain the "whys" of your decisions. Jonas Salk said, "Good parents give their children roots and wings. Roots to know where home is, wings to fly away and exercise what's been taught them." Always keep in mind that affirmation is a building and strengthening process. By establishing confidence in them through your constant positive input in their lives, you create in them the ability to empathize and speak positively into the lives of their hurting peers.

The Instructional Process: The good parent guides the child.

It is imperative we develop in our children crystal clear priorities in life. These priorities include a strong work ethic, fulfilling their obligations and commitments, as well as learning how to behave around and interact with other people.

Our children need chores to do around the house, but we don't help them build good habits or an understanding of their value as a contributing member of a unified family by giving them jobs they are incapable of doing. When we show them how to do it, then check back on them to make sure the job is getting done, we help them grow into their roles and find satisfaction and fulfillment in jobs done well.

Teach them punctuality and train them to schedule their time for the most productivity. Make sure they do their homework first before any recreational time. Don't allow procrastination. Have them pick up their toys (even big kids) and return them to the proper place when they are finished playing with them. This is especially true when they are at someone else's house. If they played with them, they should pick them up—even if others don't help. Rough playing should be reserved for the outdoors. Don't allow running in the house or jumping on the furniture. This kind of behavior breeds disrespect for property and insensitivity to the expression of good manners in various social environments.

Teach them social graces. Have them extend their hand when being introduced to others, with a cordial greeting, "Hello, I'm pleased to meet you. I'm _____." Answer the telephone with, "Hello, this is the Titus residence, Larry speaking." "Who's this?" is not acceptable. When calling others, your children should identify themselves first. Teach them to wait until everyone is served before eating.

Dads, lead the way in making sure your family eats together. The table becomes a perfect place to instill family values, instruction on table manners, and consideration for others. I will devote an entire chapter to manners later in the book. It's a topic tragically neglected in our casual cultural environment. My wife, Devi, has an incredible teaching on this subject in her book, *The Table Experience*. Copies can be purchased on our web site: www.kingdomglobal.com.

Allow only one "sleeping-in" day per week. If you worship on Sunday, Saturday's a perfect day for that. Teach them their responsibility to the other family members to remember birthdays and Christmas with cards and gifts. Always have them write their own special "love note" inside the card. Check up on what your kids are reading, and always have lots of good reading material around the house for them. Expose them to many different styles of art and music. Give them a Bible they can understand, and help them read it daily.

Don't allow sports to become the only priority in a child's life, no matter how gifted the child might be. If balance and responsibility are to be nurtured in the child, sports should come after schoolwork as well as responsibilities to home and family. Also, set a limit on the number of sports or outside activities throughout the year. Don't give children gifts that they should have to work for and earn themselves. Otherwise they will never learn responsibility. They should at least be able to contribute something to their new bike, new video game, and such. This is especially true the older they get. Expose your children to good influences and positive role models. Separate them from bad influences and negative role models. Don't allow them to speak publicly in an accusatory fashion to others or to criticize others in private. Obtain a social security number for each child. Open a savings account in their names and teach your children the value of money and the habit of responsibly building savings.

Finally, monitor the time spent watching television and playing video games. The internet can be dangerous for children. Limit their recreational time spent on the computer. Absolutely keep yourself informed about your child's internet activity and history. Know which sites they visit. Make no bones about monitoring their net activity.

The parent who makes, leads, restores, and guides his child will raise a remarkable son or daughter.

Results: The "Psalm 23 Child"

The parent who makes, leads, restores, and guides his child will raise a remarkable son or daughter. The results can be found in the final three verses of Psalm 23.

There will be an absence of fear in the child's life. "Even though I walk through the valley of the shadow of death I will fear no evil."

They will become winners over their enemies. "You prepare a table before me in the presence of my enemies."

God *anoints* your children. "You anoint my head with oil."

***Goodness and love* (mercy) will follow them throughout their lives.** "Surely goodness and love [mercy] will follow me all the days of my life."

My prayer is that your family will be exceptional in every way. I pray that your children, like Daniel, will be *ten times better* than those the world produces (Dan. 1:20).

A young Israeli warrior made a major decision more than twelve centuries before Christ. In front of the millions of people he had just led into the promised land, Joshua declared, "But as for me and my house, we will serve the Lord" (Josh. 24:15b). That's the same decision I made for my family before my children were ever born. Today every child and grandchild serves and worships God.

Fathers, make that same decision today for you and your family! Before continuing on with the next chapter, right now kneel before God the Father, and Jesus Christ, your Lord, and declare out loud, "As for me and my house, we will serve the Lord."

DIGGING YOUR DIGS

DEVI AND I RETURNED home late one night from an international trip to discover the front door of our house standing wide open. There was a foot of snow on the ground, and it was freezing cold. Due to the late hour, it was obvious the door had been open quite a while. By the time I parked the car and walked into the living room, I was already estimating the cost of the heating oil. It would be huge! But, if that wasn't enough to make my oil boil, what I saw next was more than enough. Curled up and sound asleep on our living room sofa and chairs were three of the neighborhood dogs. They were warm, cozy, and relaxed, and I was uptight, cold, and livid. When I switched on the lights, the mutts merely stretched, yawned, and looked at us through sleepy eyes. Truly, it was a Three Dog Night.

The college students living with us hadn't taken the two minutes to check that the doors were locked and everything was secure before going to bed.

I'm sharing this story to illustrate a very important principle in the Word of God. This is the principle of *stewardship*. The *Merriam-Webster Dictionary* defines *stewardship* as, "the conducting, supervising, or managing of something, *especially* the careful and responsible management of something entrusted to one's care."

We had entrusted our home and possessions to our young adult residents. However, they did not do a good job stewarding our belongings. They were negligent. Not only were they negligent, they were presumptuous. We learned the next morning that they had thrown a big party for their entire family. Out came our best china, crystal, and sterling silver for the festive occasion. It never occurred to them to check with us before hosting this lavish affair. Fortunately, nothing was broken. While the neighborhood dogs might have been grateful, we were not.

Stewardship is an obligation and a responsibility in many of our relationships. It might be the fiduciary duty we assume over someone's estate or trust fund. If we work with not-for-profit organizations or oversee property or simply stay in someone's home, we become stewards. As was the case with our young college students, it could be the stewardship attendant with living in our home. It certainly applies to the use of borrowed items. Stewardship is the act of assuming personal responsibility for the proper care and management of something placed into our hands. Whatever that "something" is, it's not mine. It belongs to someone else and it has been entrusted into my care.

More than eighty young men and a few young women have lived in our home over the years. It became obvious early on that most of these young adults did not come into our lives with a fully developed sense of stewardship. The three dogs that took over our living room and some of our young guests shared a few bad habits—drop in for a while, stretch out in the living room, and wish somebody else would close that front door.

It didn't naturally occur to our young "sons" that the lawn needed to be cut, their bedroom needed to be kept neat and clean, dishes needed to be washed, floors needed to be vacuumed, the house occasionally needed some minor repairs or painting. Oh, and the car might need to be washed and filled with gasoline when returned. And, say, how do you work that washer and dryer? In addition to our investment in their spiritual lives, Devi and I have made an enormous investment year in and out as we trained young men and women in the discipline of stewardship.

Devi and I have had to conceal smiles as we later observed our young charges when they married and began to manage their own homes. Suddenly, their houses were neat as a pin, their cars were washed and waxed, their lawns were manicured, and their kids looked like they had just jumped off the pages of a Nordstrom catalog. My wife and I proudly take credit for their transformations into good stewards. So, in this chapter, I want to concentrate on how to "dig your digs." That's Titus-slang for how we practice a servant-headship type of stewardship of our homes.

How to Dig Your Digs

Men, let's do some groundwork and focus our thinking on stewardship. We believe our homes, cars, furniture, clothes, jewelry, and toys are "our" possessions. Yet, they really aren't ours. David tells us in Psalm 24:1, "The earth is the LORD'S, and everything in it, the world, and all who live in it." I'd say that covers just about everything. It all belongs to God and those things which God places into our hands are resources to be cared for and properly managed. They are material goods given to us by our loving Heavenly Father for our convenience, welfare, and enjoyment. God's requirement is that we exercise proper stewardship over these things.

There are many scriptural examples of stewardship. Notably, in the Old Testament, Joseph was made steward over Potiphar's house. In a very real way, Joseph was a prototypical Teleios Man. He was completed by God's will and purpose through a series of much less-than-perfect situations which situated him in the perfect place at the perfect time with the mindset of faithful trust to bring life and hope to the whole population of his part of the world. Later, he was made the second most powerful man in Egypt, answering only to Pharaoh himself.

In the New Testament, Jesus speaks of the dishonest steward in Luke 16. This man was accused of mismanaging his master's possessions. Because of his mismanagement, he was removed from his position as steward. Paul tells the Corinthian church, "Moreover it is required in stewards, that a man be found faithful" (1 Cor. 4:2, KJV).

The Secret of Good Stewardship

I place a high value on my home, car, and other material goods, not because they are my possessions but because these things have been entrusted into my care by God. I want everything I do with them to be a good reflection on me, my family, Jesus, and my Father in heaven who owns everything. I am a steward of that portion of God's property he has entrusted to me. It's critical that I do a faithful job because eventually the Owner is going to require from me an accounting for my stewardship. My reward will be commensurate with my effort, my integrity, and my results. Guys, remember: we're all going to have to give an accounting!

How can a willing, motivated man become a good steward? Here's a key thought. Act as though whatever is in your care is actually something you own. Good stewardship is a correct attitude about the resources in our hands. As well, we must recognize we are living witnesses to the unbelievers around us. The way we conduct our affairs, manage our homes, and take care of the other material goods God has placed into our hands truly represents our Christianity.

Good stewardship is a correct attitude about the resources in our hands.

Really, the effectiveness of our stewardship is very visible and evident, isn't it? Our houses, cars, and yards immediately show our attitude of care. It all shapes up as a real indicator of our maturity and sense of responsibility.

Don't Call Me Mr. Fix-It!

You may be a real handy guy around the house, able to do wiring, carpentry, and maybe even some plumbing. Or, you could be like me, mechanically challenged when it comes to repairs. Either way, I think we ought to take a shot at learning how to master at least the small repairs which often become necessary around the house. However, I must confess that, early in our marriage, I told Devi the best way to get a repair done was to pick up the phone.

I love our home, I love the way Devi decorates it, and I'm proud to bring to bring people home with me. I just don't do "fix-it" that well. You might say I'm the Tim Allen of the home world. I can do the grunt labor, but I'm an accident waiting to happen if there's a problem requiring skill in electrical, plumbing, or carpentry work. I do not exaggerate. I've made serious mistakes when I've tried to do even quasi-skilled work. But, I do like giving it a try, even though the learning process has occasionally cost me more in time and money, but the short-term aggravation has long-term positive potential. Let me take you on a walk through the Titus household. You'll hear some good stories about my handiwork.

There was the electrical fixture I installed upside down. I wondered aloud how the manufacturers were able to get away with such dumb assembly instructions. I muttered, "They ought to fire the guy who designed this piece of junk." Then I thought, "Why, for a person to screw in the light bulb he'd have to be standing in the attic." Obviously the "light" hadn't gone on in my head. You get the idea.

I once mounted an ironing board wall bracket with great precision. Stepping back to admire my work, I noted the holes for the molly bolts I'd drilled were too low. I'd placed the hanger several inches below the height of the ironing board.

I cut a hole in the wallpaper one time for an outlet receptacle while the paper was still on the floor. When we hung the wallpaper, the hole was on the wrong side and four feet higher than the receptacle.

My crowning "achievement" involved an exploding garbage dumpster which left my eyebrows singed and curled, and I was given an instant afro. It burned for hours—the dumpster that is. When the fire trucks came, my son eagerly told the firemen that it was his dad who had used the dumpster as an incinerator. You have to love a kid like that. He'd been taught honesty as a strict ethic.

Regardless of my bumbling efforts, I make sure the household projects get done. And, I have had some successes. I keep the grass cut and the shrubs trimmed. I help Devi with landscaping. I keep the house painted inside and out. I keep the car washed and waxed. I make it a point to help my wife with vacuuming, dusting, and general cleaning around the house. Sound's exciting, yes? Well, if not, sorry guys. It all falls under the responsibility of stewardship and sacrificial servant-leadership.

Get the Kids Digging the Digs

Let me just make some quick comments about involving our kids in stewardship.

The best way to teach children stewardship principles is to make them responsible for the care of their toys and clothes from an early age. Have them make their beds and pick up their toys after they play with them. They'll learn from these small duties. We owe our kids this, and if *we* don't teach them, they'll learn in harder ways in later years.

Often, I've seen expensive toys left outside in the elements. Some kids are never taught how to care for their own property. In teen years, the discarded toys might be replaced with cars and jet skies, but the lack of care remains the same. That's called poor stewardship, and it finds its final consequence when the teens become parents and repeat the same pattern.

It is vitally important that dads and moms don't do everything for their children. Young people—from early ages on up, as their development allows for increased responsibility—need to learn to wash, dry, fold, and iron clothes. They need to make their beds, pick up their toys, return their clothes to the closet on hangers, toss the dirty clothes into hampers, return baseball mitts and basketballs to the proper storage place, and wash the dishes on occasion or as a part of regular chores. We can help them fix broken toys. Then, when they get older, they'll have the skills I don't have and can hang light fixtures and ironing boards.

A most important application of stewardship relates to borrowed things. We need to treat borrowed property as if it were our own—or even better. If something is borrowed, return it immediately after using it or when you said you would. If you break it, replace it. When you borrow a vehicle, top off the tank and wash it. Return borrowed or loaned property better than when you received it. This is a classy action that speaks much louder than your words ever could. Remember it.

We humans are led by our models. When we model good stewardship, our children watch and learn, and they remember much more than we might think. Our neighbors make judgments about us and compare our actions against our professions of faith. One of the best ways for our families to "speak" for Jesus in our neighborhoods is to demonstrate genuine respect for the personal property of others around us.

Our Heavenly Digs

Jesus told the disciples in John 14 that in his Father's house "are many rooms." The King James Version says "many mansions." He went on to tell them he was going there to prepare a place for them. You can get a better picture of what these heavenly "digs" look like when you read the final two chapters in the Book of Revelation.

The city itself is pretty spectacular. Streets are made of gold, the gates are pearl, the foundations are overlaid with the most beautiful gems, and the river and fountains are similarly spectacular. The entire city is one fabulous gated community measuring fourteen hundred miles *cubed*! John must have really struggled to intellectually grasp what he was looking at. He says in Revelation 21:11, "It shone with the glory of God, and its brilliance was like that of a very precious jewel, like jasper, clear as crystal." God's house is a big house, and it's clear he designed then built it with beauty, extravagance, excellence, and opulence.

Our earthly "mansion"—our home—should be held in as much esteem as God holds his, and we should emulate his excellence of stewardship. I think we often struggle with this issue of excellence in our lives. What's the big deal? Well, here's the big deal. God doesn't do anything half-way. Everything he does, he does with divine excellence. It's his nature, indeed his very character, which is reflected in what he does. *God is as interested in the excellence of our thinking and character as he is in the outcomes of our stewardship.* In other words, our stewardship will reflect our true character. God wants his sons to exhibit the same fully developed character he exhibits. That is the Teleios Way—the way of spiritual maturity which is exhibited in completion in Christ—both inward and outer evidence of growth

...our stewardship will reflect our true character.

Character is built through faithfulness. Faithfulness requires consistency. I believe stewardship is reflected in our attention to the details—the little things. "You were faithful with a few things, I will put you in charge of many things" (Matt. 25:21, NASB).

I want my yard to honor God. I want my garage to be a testimony to him. I want the garbage cans, tools, and equipment stored and organized. I want the driveway hosed down. I want the windows washed. I want the gutters cleaned. I want the burned out light bulbs replaced. I want my house to reflect the awesome Lord I serve. I want my car to be a good reflection on the owner, Jesus Christ. I want my mansion to look like his—prepared!

I earnestly wish for those reading this to understand and internalize a very important principle: take care of the details. Do not be above dealing with these small items. You will be rewarded for your efforts, I promise. It's an observable truth in the history of our world.

Since Jesus went away two thousand years ago to prepare a place for us, I suspect it's looking pretty good by now. Don't you think? If God takes seriously the appointments and accoutrements for the mansion he is preparing for us, surely we should do the same for our mansions down here. So, get out the mower and weed whacker, get out the hoses, get those pruning shears oiled up. Get out the ladders and garbage bags. Pry open a can of paint and...go for it!

I cannot overstate the value I have placed on my "mansion" over the years. Whether it was the one-bedroom studio apartment we had when first married or our two-bedroom concrete block apartment with those cold concrete floors, or the three-storied home we live in now, Devi and I treated them all as our mansions. The yards, exterior, interior, garage, and décor were and are a reflection of my attitude toward and love for Jesus, my wife, and my family. I want to do the best I can to bring honor and enjoyment for those I cherish most.

Whether your house is a hut, a cabin, a condominium, a simple rental, or a palatial residence, it's the earthly mansion God has provided for you, so steward it well. Remember, a home doesn't need to be ostentatious or pretentious to be a mansion. It just needs to receive a high standard of care. In fact, it is better to have a smaller home meticulously cared for than a larger one that is neglected.

What Shall We Do about It?

Here are five ideas I've listed to just get the ball rolling and think about stewardship around your house.

1.   Make a list of the qualities and features that you consider most important about your home.
2.   Now take note of any maintenance or repair issues that aren't currently being managed well.
3.   Make a prioritized "to-do" list of things in your home that need to be improved, repaired, painted, or hauled away.
4.   Write a list of chores for which you've not assumed full responsibility.
5.   Commit to make a change. Share these things with your wife so she can hold you accountable to see that you follow through with your plans—ouch!

Turning Houses into Homes

What's the critical element needed to turn a house into a home? You guessed it: people! It's the human activity, closeness, communication, and warmth that remodels a cold container into a welcoming living environment. What a difference there is between entering an empty house with no power, lights, furniture, or fixtures, or any sounds of life and family and entering one with the lights on, rooms beautifully furnished, rugs on the floor, pictures on the wall, but most importantly of all, the sounds of human interaction!

When Mom is trying to get a meal on the table, the kids are running around, the dog is barking, the T.V. is on, and Dad is still outside mowing the lawn, there's life in the house! It is a home. So, I want to share a few thoughts on stewardship in the *home*.

In our forty-six years of marriage, Devi and I have hosted hundreds, probably thousands, of people in our home, and we've found no better place to disciple people. We dig our digs. We love our home, and we enjoy hosting people there as often as we can. Home is where the action is. In spite of the dumb things I do around the house once in a while, over the years Devi and I have turned our "digs" into a home. We place an incredibly high value on our home life. Home is more than just a place to hang our hat or to spend a few hours sleeping at night. As Devi says, "It's a haven of rest and a sanctuary of love." And believe me, she knows how to make it just that. It's Devi's personality that has turned our house into a home. I think that's the case in most homes. Many wives are able to add the warmth, the caring touch, the thoughtful extras, and the touch of class to the décor that gives everything that special feeling.

It's important for men to really understand the passion and motivation our wives have as they work to turn our houses into homes. It's how God hardwired them. Women have a natural "nesting" instinct. They naturally care about the environment they live in. Women want beautiful things around them, and they work creatively and hard to make things nice. Guys, on the other hand, can generally live in a cave. Running water? Microwaves? Toilets? Air fresheners? Drapes? Get real! Give me a stick, a piece of meat, and a fire. I can sleep on the ground and pull some leaves over me if I get cold. Of course, for our current generation, this might be a little over the top, but you get the idea.

It's going to be trouble, husbands, if you are insensitive to the importance your wives place on the environment of home. They take their nest very seriously. For you guys thinking of marriage, it would be a good idea to rivet your attention to this point. I've seen so many wives dispirited by husbands who wouldn't mow the lawn, rake the leaves, clean the garage, or paint the shutters. Let's not even mention their unwillingness to do the dishes, help cook a meal, vacuum a floor, or clean the toilets once in a while.

Wives experience a real sense of exasperation when their husbands take zero interest in the home's condition and décor. Gentlemen, I can tell you from a lot of counseling experience, wives would definitely like to get more out of you than the stereotypical, monosyllabic, caveman grunt. Homes that should be filled with love often become danger zones of incredible female frustration. Marriages that should be totally in sync can become battlegrounds, with the wife reduced to nagging just to get a few things done. It's an embarrassment to women in these situations. All too often men seem oblivious to the problem. Why is this lack of caring on the part of husbands an embarrassment to the wives? Well, wives want their homes to be a beautiful living environment for their families and a warm, inviting place to entertain friends. I think women often exhibit the superior sense of stewardship in this area compared to men. And that is not right!

My usual forbearing, non-confrontational personality could ideally become more aggressive at this point. I'm serious. I'm very slow in confronting men on these issues. But nothing galls me more than observing a man's pattern of sitting and watching television or surfing the net for hours while his yard remains uncared for and home projects remain undone. It really gets to me when I witness the incredible disrespect husbands can sometimes show to their wives' desire to create a nurturing home atmosphere. Men, something is desperately wrong in our sense of values if we can be content with leisure and inactivity while our wives slave to make us comfortable. Let me lay aside delicacy and diplomacy long enough to say, "Repent, get off your posteriors, and get moving!"

We do well to carry the same sense of pride and value in our home as our wives do. Many wives take a great sense of self and satisfaction in the role of keeper and nurturer in a home. If it's her "department," then I'm her provider and muscle to ensure that the work gets done, and we demonstrate Christ's sacrificial love when we try to get things done to our wives' standards. This may seem like a foreign concept to some of us "net surfers," but there it is nonetheless. And, make sure that your children develop that same sense of love for the home as well. We reflect an elevated sense of stewardship when we assume our responsibilities as men. It's more than just the stewardship we must show over *things*. Indeed, it's the stewardship found in supporting our wives in all that God has called them to do. So, guys, help them turn a house into a home. You and everyone around you will benefit!

My son, Aaron, recently emailed me an article from an unnamed author which I think demonstrates the point nicely. Here goes:

> After the long months of cold and winter, we will soon be coming up to summer and BBQ season. Therefore, it is important to refresh

your memory on the etiquette of this sublime outdoor cooking as it's the only type of cooking a real man will do, probably because there is an element of danger involved.

When a man volunteers to do the BBQ, the following chain of events is put into motion and here's the routine:

1. The woman buys the food.
2. The woman makes the salad, prepares the vegetables, and makes dessert.
3. The woman prepares the meat for cooking, places it on a tray along with the necessary cooking utensils and sauces, and takes it to the man who is lounging beside the grill—cold drink in hand. (Now, here comes the important part.)
4. THE MAN PLACES THE MEAT ON THE GRILL.
5. The woman goes inside to organize the plates and cutlery.
6. The woman comes out to tell the man that the meat is burning. (He thanks her and asks if she will bring another cold drink while he deals with the situation.)
7. THE MAN TAKES THE MEAT OFF THE GRILL AND HANDS IT TO THE WOMAN.
8. The woman prepares the plates, salad, bread, utensils, napkins, sauces and brings them to the table.
9. After eating, the woman clears the table and does the dishes. Then, most important of all—
10. Everyone PRAISES the MAN and THANKS HIM for his cooking efforts.
11. The man asks the woman how she enjoyed "her night off." And, upon seeing her annoyed reaction, concludes that there's just no pleasing some women.

Husbands, and wannabe husbands—our stewardship responsibility goes beyond barbecuing burgers and really extends to our full partnership in creating an orderly environment in the home. By supporting our wives, we demonstrate our love for them and our respect for their natural desire to have a beautiful and inviting place for their family and anyone else invited in. It will also nurture a peaceful and harmonious atmosphere creating a safe place for all kinds of ministry.

Homes: the First Church Buildings

If I understand my church history correctly, in the first century or two of the church, when believers weren't meeting in the temple courts, people always met in homes. This is narrated in Acts 2:46 and 5:42, Romans 16:5, Colossians 4:15, 1 Corinthians 16:19, and Philemon 2. The home is the church in its purest form, or at least it's supposed to be. Every husband and wife should desire that their home to be modeled after the house of God—the church—in proper order and full of peace and love. The husband and wife are the pastors, and the children are the congregation. It is to be a place of worship and praise, teaching, correction, and instruction in righteousness. The husband and wife should be the perfect model of Christ and the church. Your children are your first disciples. There is no need attempting to disciple others until you have first made disciples of your own family members.

What makes the home so important is that it forms the foundation for the larger church. The corporate church is only as strong as the individual homes, the foundational church.

God Has a Home Too

God is the ultimate homebody. Jesus commented he was going to Father's house to prepare a place for us. First of all, what makes God's house a home is exactly what makes our house a home. He lives there! Evidently he likes a big house with a lot of rooms because he's got a big and growing family who will be living in his home with him. In fact, think of this: he is preparing the eternal accommodations for his Son and his Son's bride! If that doesn't get you thinking, you'd better check your pulse!

Here's another profound realization: at the same time Jesus and the Father occupy heaven, they are making their home in us right now by the agency of the Holy Spirit. We, the church, are currently God's temple—his home here on earth. Jesus said in John 14:23, "If anyone loves me, he will obey my teaching. My Father will love him, and we will come to him and make *our home* with him" (emphasis added). The word *home* in 14:23 is the same word translated as "house" in 14:2.

Men, our families are the "mansion," the dwelling place, of God during the current church age. Not only does God want you to live in his mansion in eternity, he's living in yours right now. What makes your body—your soul's physical house—a home is the fact God lives there! And, God is currently applying the same spiritual stewardship principles in our lives he wishes us to apply in our earthly homes. He's washing us, polishing us, trimming us, and renewing us to bring us into conformity with the beauty of his character. We do well to think a while on that one too.

John tells us in Revelation 21:3a, "And I heard a loud voice from the throne saying, 'Now the dwelling of God is with men, and he will live with them.'" This will be when the New Jerusalem comes down out of heaven and there is a new heaven and new earth. I think it's virtually impossible to grasp this idea with our mortal minds. God's plan has always been to live with us. John tells us at the end of this chapter that he did not see a temple in the city because the Lord God Almighty and the Lamb were there. They *are* the temple. There will be no need for light from the sun or moon because their glory will light the city. Talk about turning a house into a home!

I can never understand the man who wants to always be away from his home. Without us, our wives, and the kids, our houses are just empty shells full of stuff. Turning that house into a home is the tip of the stewardship spear. If we apply stewardship principles diligently to everything God has placed in our hands, we will see material objects shine with his grace in our lives. Our homes are used by God as his plan for us is put into place.

Men, please think about this and then act. Your home deserves your best stewardship efforts. Do this, and your rewards will be substantial. I guarantee it.

And while you're thinking about this, I'll be trying to start my lawn mower. I made a little adjustment last week. The thing hasn't run right since…

Peace Stealers

Your wallet was on the kitchen counter the last time you looked, but now it's gone. Your keys aren't where they're supposed to be. You've misplaced your Bible. You call your cell phone in hopes of hearing a ring and then tracking it down. You thought you left your coat hanging on the back of the chair, but it's not there. You can't find your tools. Does this sound familiar?

You see, in nearly every moment of every day there are a thousand little trifles that can destroy your peace. Hypertension, irritability, and anxiety cloud your mind and usurp a peaceful and productive state. Without bringing order and organization into your daily life, you cannot experience the fullness of Christ's peace.

Let's look further into this. Guys, I want you at peace. Then you can work on other important things in your lives.

In the early years of our ministry, Devi and I traveled a lot. At every stop I would forget something—shoes, jackets, underwear, books, toothbrushes, and countless other items. *Finally, I started making mental hooks.* "When leaving a hotel room, don't pick up your keys until you've checked all the drawers, bathroom counters, and closets." Just the simple rule of using my keys as a memory check helped cut down considerably on lost and left items. This is just one of the many practical, effective "hooks" I can recommend.

I wish I could tell you that clothes are the worst thing I ever lost. But that wouldn't be true. On one outing, I lost our son in the heart of San Francisco's Chinatown.

The Lost Kid

Devi and I were shopping in downtown San Francisco one summer. We turned our attention back towards our trailing four-year-old son only to discover him missing. We were panicked and horror stuck. "Honey, where's Aaron?"

"I don't know; I thought you had him."

"The last I saw him he was with you."

"With *me*? The last time I saw him he was with you." You see, I still had a tad amount of defensiveness left in me. What a relief that I am now delivered...

Where do you look for a little boy in that huge city? How much time had passed since we'd last seen him? The adrenaline and fear were setting in and our minds were spinning like pinwheels.

At that moment, a policeman walked into the store with our son. "Does anyone recognize this little boy?" The terror turned to humiliation. We were the world's worst parents in the eyes of that cop.

Should I tell you about the time we locked up the church and drove home forgetting that Aaron was asleep on the front pew of the church? We returned forty minutes later to find him still fast asleep. I wonder if he has any lingering emotional scars?

Now what I forget the most is my cell phone. A cell phone is *much less* important than a child, of course, so I consider this to be significant progress, but the nuisance factor is fairly high, though. Thankfully, the horrified fear and mortified humiliation are not issues with the inanimate objects I misplace. After leaving without it a couple of times, I decided to start another "hook." Now every night when I plug in my cell phone, I put my keys beside it. I can't start my car in the morning without my keys, and I don't pick up my keys without having my cell phone. I do the same thing when eating out. If I take my cell phone out of my pocket, I will put my car keys beside it to keep from forgetting it. Just a simple habit makes life so much easier, removes confusion, and contributes to a more peaceful, less stressful mind-set with which to start the day.

Oh, and another thing: When I need to take an item with me, I will either set it in front of the door or put it in the car as soon as I think of it. I'll trip over it on the way out, or I'll take it with me. Now, I seldom leave things. So, fellows, if I can learn to order my world, so can you.

Peace Stealers

See if you can relate to the following "peace stealers."

✓ You're meeting your client in ten minutes. You just remembered that your gas tank is empty. It will take an extra ten minutes to get to the gas station, then you'll need to fumble around with your gas card and the pump. You'll be late for your appointment and since you forgot your cell, you can't call. There goes your peace.

✓ You had to be at the city park at 5:00 p.m. to coach your daughter's soccer game, but you tried to squeeze in a few more appointments before you left the office. It still would have worked out OK, but at the last minute you had an emergency phone call, and it lasted longer than you expected. Now you can't possibly make it in time, and the team will have to wait until you get there. There goes your peace.

✓ It's Sunday morning; you and your wife overslept and now you're running late for church. You would have still had time to make it, but just as you were heading out the door you discovered that you were missing one of the kid's shoes. Naturally, you yelled at your wife for not knowing where the shoe was. It's not *your* fault if she can't find the kids' shoes. And as your trek to the car began, your wife discovered that the baby has filled his diaper. There goes your peace, your wife's peace, and the baby's peace.

✓ On your way to a new couple's house for dinner, you realize too late that you forgot to bring the scrap of paper you'd used to write down the directions. They asked you to be there at 6:00 p.m. sharp, but now you're going to be late because you've got to return home and get the directions. You could have called them, but their phone number is written on the same paper. You don't have their address or phone number, and you've also lost peace. You think maybe your wife should have handled these details. In fact, you *know* she should have…

✓ It's just two days before Christmas. You'd intended to buy your wife's gift before now, but basically you procrastinated, and the tension is mounting. You think, *That does it; today I'm going to stop on the way home from work.* After standing in line ten minutes, you hear the clerk tell you, "Oh, I'm sorry, but we ran out of them last night." Your fall-back plan is to stop on Christmas Eve at the other store that carries the same item. You'll have time if you leave early from work. There goes your peace, just as you were preparing to celebrate the birth of the Prince of Peace.

What the Word Says

There's an incredibly practical scripture found in 1 Corinthians 14:33a. The Apostle Paul makes it clear that "For God is not a God of disorder but of peace." Notice that the opposite of disorder and confusion is peace.

When things are brought into order, peace is the result.

When things are brought into order, peace is the result. You know it, guys, and I know it. Disorganization will always result in confusion and a lack of peace.

The purpose of this chapter isn't to heap condemnation on anyone for a lack of organization. You feel enough condemnation without my help. Rather, my purpose is to give you a wake-up call (with my cell phone) and convict and encourage you to bring structure and order to those things in your life that are sloppy and out of order. Making order out of chaos is part of God's power to perfect, to complete, his purpose in nature—including human nature.

Every area of mismanagement produces confusion and removes peace. What's optimal—bringing order to your world or living without peace? One of man's deepest needs is to have domestic tranquility, so the first option is the obvious pick, but God's order and his peace don't come to us automatically. We have to choose to participate, to pursue it, to work at making it a reality in our lives—day by day.

You're going to have to put on your management hat. This will be like the practice and drills you might have run through in school sports. It's work.

In Mayor Rudolph Giuliani's book on leadership, he quoted the architect Ludwig Mies van der Rohe from the *New York Herald Tribune*: "God is in the details." Giuliani followed the quotation with, "Amen to that." He went on to say, "Knowing the 'small' details of a large system leaves a leader open to charges of micromanaging. But understanding how something works is not only a leader's responsibility; it also makes him or her better able to let people do their jobs."*

If you think that Mayor Giuliani did a great job in managing New York City, take a wider look to see what God does administrating the universe.

How God Orders His World

Nothing should provide more encouragement for you than to know how God orders his world. He's the most organized person in the universe. He's also a genius engineer. Nothing escapes his attention. The entire universe runs in perfect harmony with laws that he has fixed and rules that he has made.

Before suggesting some possible rules for bringing order into your private world, I'd like to point out some of God's organizational strategies.

God Numbers Everything

The Bible carefully points out that God numbers the stars. He quantifies the days, months, years, and the span or our lives. He counts the fruit of the Spirit, the gifts of the Spirit, the years of the tribulation period, the foundations, gates, and cubic feet of the Celestial City, the number of the

---

* Giuliani, *Leadership*, 46.

tribes of Israel, and even how many from the twelve tribes will be sealed during the tribulation period.

The new converts who were saved and added to the church at Pentecost were numbered (three thousand) as well as the names of the nations that were represented at the Feast. The disciples were numbered. When one fell out, another disciple was added to the number, so the total could be brought up again to twelve.

The days of creation were numbered as well as the days of the flood and even how many animals were loaded on the ark. God numbered the years of each of the antediluvian patriarchs and threw in for good measure the age of the oldest of the oldies—Methuselah—who kicked the bucket at the ripe old age of 969. All I can say is, at that age, who cares about who's counting? I've even been known to be unable to remember the ages of my kids. It's a good thing I have my wife to rely on for information like that.

The Old Testament enumerates the soldiers who fought in battle, how many died, how many were routed, how much spoil was taken, and how long it took to fight the battle. It lists the names, years, length of reign, and other numerous details of the lives of the kings of Israel and Judah. One entire book is called "Numbers" because everything in it is numbered. What's more, God even lists the names along with the genealogies.

As if God didn't have enough things to number, Jesus says in Matthew 10:30 that he numbers the hairs of our heads. Men, some of us are losing hair daily, yet God keeps the count!

The bottom line is that God numbers everything and knows at all times every single thing that is going on his universe. God never forgets the score of a game. It's no wonder that he's currently seated with his Son sitting relaxed at his side. Everything has already been quantified and accounted for.

Then there's me. I run around like a chicken with my head cut off, trying to get things organized and properly administered. I struggle to remember where I put something or what I did with it. Here are some of the strategies that work for me...

Larry's Rules of Order

- Everything has a place, and it's out of place if it's not in its place.

- Designate a place for everything in your home. Decide on a key place, a coat place, a spare change place, a hat place, a hammer place, a blue shirt place, a lawn tool place, an underwear place, and a socks place By the way, the designated "socks place" cannot be on the floor where you threw them last night when you came home from work. When everything has an exact place, your home can run efficiently. You must adhere to the rules that you set. No cheating!

- Have a master calendar where all the events and activities for the family members are recorded. Don't make plans until you check the master calendar. This can reduce confusion and time conflicts.

- Don't make decisions until you check with the boss. Who's the boss? Whoever needs to be informed before you make a final decision. In your marriage, it's your wife. For your wife, it's you. In the church, it's your pastor. At your job, it's your supervisor. For your future, it's the Big Boss—God!

- Don't Procrastinate. Do the things you don't want to do first. Do the easy, enjoyable things last. Anything you put off for "later" will cause you problems "later." Guys, you and I both know this stuff is not too basic to review. We all need to observe these simple disciplines.

- In time management, give priority to your home. It's easy to put work, the church, and social events ahead of your home. Unless the stewardship of our homes is part of our number one priority of servant-leadership, everything else will be out of balance.

- Buy the proper tools for every task or maintenance problem. It's difficult to do a job well with inferior tools. Once you invest in them, you will always have them available when you need them, and the quality of your work will be higher.

- Make a practice of keeping "to do" lists. As it relates to work, if you'll make the list the night before, you're far more likely to accomplish your goals for the following day. Computer software is great for maintaining a task menu that can keep you on track and on schedule.

- Take notes on everything of importance—from quotes to quips, to anecdotes, to reminders of important ideas or events. There's a reason some of the top business and professional schools teach the necessity of and effectiveness of documentation. Abraham Lincoln was an enthusiastic note taker. Many of the ideas for the Gettysburg Address had been written in advance on small scraps of paper and stashed in his hat band. The night before his speech, he emptied his hat and wrote the historic words. This makes you want to go out and buy a big hat, doesn't it?

- Have a designated Sabbath day of rest. God wants you and your family to have a day to refresh your body, soul, and spirit. After you've worked for six days, you must have a time to regroup and regain perspective. An ox in the ditch was a good reason to break the Sabbath in Jesus's day, but too many oxen in too many ditches on too many consecutive Sabbaths will wear you down and destroy your peace. God knows that we must have time to rest, replenish, and renew. And there is no better reason for us to rest than the knowledge that both God and Jesus are currently at rest and have been for quite some time.

- Maintain appropriate files for important paper work such as insurance papers, income tax information, financial records, deeds, birth and wedding certificates, and a will. You'll save time and frustration.

- Invest in hooks, filing cabinets, plastic container bins, shelves, tabs, labels and hangers, so that everything in your home, garage, and office can be contained, stored, identified, categorized, and properly controlled.

- Make a list of everything that is not organized and make a plan to bring it into administrative excellence. Use some of the categories and places I've listed below:

  - ❑ Home
  - ❑ Garage
  - ❑ Work place/office
  - ❑ Closet
  - ❑ Tools
  - ❑ Household supplies
  - ❑ Replacement items
  - ❑ Chest of drawers

Time Management

Time is a funny concept. We always say things like, "Man, time is flying!" or "Wow, my time just got away from me today!" No matter what we say, time is always moving, flying, or running. It never stops, delays, or halts. It won't wait on us, and it absolutely, definitely will not alter its pace to meet our demands. It is not on *your* schedule. Time management is about taking something uncontrollable and controlling it. Like a kite, floating away in the wind, you must quickly grab that string and guide it. But enjoy the kite and the wind as you do it!

Here are a few tips to help manage your time:

- Factor in everything! This is simply making a time budget. Don't forget that putting on your shoes, walking to the car, slinging a briefcase in the backseat, and backing out of the driveway will take more than thirty seconds!

- Always give yourself lead time. You have to assign a time value to everything because everything takes time. Don't miscalculate how long it will take to do something because you missed those details and trifles that chew up time. Managing time and resources is an absolutely necessary skill. Project managers in the business world take long courses of study and use complicated software in this process of managing time. But, time management still comes down to estimation and continual revision as you learn more and more. Follow your time!

- Don't waste precious time. It's one thing to relax or take a quick break, but it could be a big problem if hours and hours in your day are being wasted. Efficiently use your time in your work. At home, put yourself to good use helping out around the house, putting things away that have been stacked or staged for storage. Do chores for your wife in advance, knowing she's pressed for time and will surely appreciate the help.

- Every day includes downtime while you wait for someone or something. I always keep a book close at hand for those extra minutes that would otherwise be wasted, or I return phone calls or review my notes. If you have a lot of free time, invest it in something! There are countless numbers of people who could use your assistance! Find someone who needs a mentor or father and spend this time with them.

- Always factor margins or time buffers into your planning in case of emergencies. Give yourself extra time—relaxing time. Don't ever leave for an appointment so that you'll arrive "just in time." Leave early. I heard someone say that leaders are always on time, and great leaders are ten minutes early.

- Coordinate projects so that you can complete several at once. If you've got to make a trip across town, list all the stops that are in close proximity. Multiple trips aren't needed if you'll do a little planning.

- I'll say it again! Make lists! Update the lists and cross off the items you've completed. Lists are simple but highly effective tools. Keep lists and keep them updated and current.

So, that's how it works. When we bring administrative and management excellence into our lives, the stress and strain of disorganization will give way to peace and composure. We can't control everything, but let's carefully organize and steward what comes into our hands.

...let's carefully organize and steward what comes into our hands.

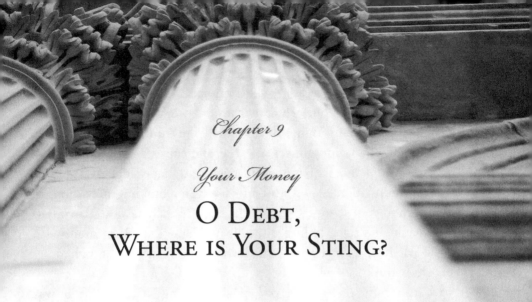

Chapter 9

Your Money

O DEBT,
WHERE IS YOUR STING?

T HE CHRISTIAN WORLD HAS trouble talking about money. Money issues have destroyed marriages, businesses, churches, and countries. Money is stored value and a medium of exchange, and we all deal with it every day of our lives. So, why is money so hard to discuss? Perhaps it's the capitalistic mentality which pervades our thinking.

What on earth am I saying?

From an early age, we are taught self-reliance and the need for a strong work ethic. We are also taught that our economic system gives us opportunity to accumulate wealth. To be sure, scripture discusses work and money.

Yet, here is where the snare is set. We begin to think that what we earn is "ours and our alone." "What's mine is mine" is thinking related to the notion of self-reliance. In other words, "I worked for it. I earned it. So, it belongs to me."

Our concern here is what God has to say about money and finances. We are NOT concerned with the mentality of unbelievers when it comes to money. Unbelievers are part of the mammon system, and the mammon system has an incredible history of self-reliance, wealth accumulation, and empire building as well as altruism, generosity, and charity.

I approach this subject from a position of real humility, because, like many of you, I've had my share of financial pain caused by faulty thinking, bad decisions, and, on occasion, sinful choices. Today, I have a humbled knowledge of many money choices that don't work and a keen appreciation and conviction for things that do work. I'm committed to principles that are biblically sound, universally true, and consistently productive.

There is a plethora of money management knowledge available to us. This information is powerful and useful for building new thought processes and then actions for finally getting our financial houses in order. Let's dive in and start dealing with this problematic topic of money. It's time we do it, and I'm always excited when we can take on a tough topic. Let's study this together.

We read in the first chapter of Daniel that King Nebuchadnezzar was looking among the Hebrew captives for young men "showing aptitude for every kind of learning, well informed, quick to understand, and qualified to serve in the king's palace" (Dan. 1:4). Later, we read in the same chapter, that God gave Daniel and his three friends "knowledge and understanding of all kinds of literature and learning." At the end of the chapter, we read, "In every matter of wisdom and understanding about which the king questioned them, he found them *ten times better* than all the magicians and enchanters in his whole kingdom" (emphasis added).

Daniel and his friends rose to incredible levels of power and authority in the Babylonian empire because of aptitude and *learning*. Incumbent upon all of us is the need to equip ourselves to be able stewards of the resources God has placed in our hands. Because there is so much "literature and learning" available in the area of Christian approaches to financial stewardship, I really want to focus on three specific money concepts which I feel provide a biblical foundation for our thinking about money. These three concepts are Giving, Debt, and Saving.

What's Mine is Not Mine

I pray we can recognize this crucial truth in the Word of God: "What's mine is really not mine; it's God's." I truly believe we cannot correctly receive or utilize the blessings of God unless we understand this and act accordingly. It must be the driving force in our thinking and behavior relating to money.

Believers quickly agree that our life, breath, and indeed our very existence all come from God (see Acts 17). But when we think about money, somehow it becomes "ours." This is really the gist of the spiritual conflict Jesus addressed in Matthew 6:24. He said, "You cannot serve both *God and money*" (emphasis added).

In this verse, Jesus clarifies what happens when we fall into the trap of thinking money is "ours." His focus *is* ownership but not *our* ownership. The real issue is who or what owns us? Does our heart belong to *money or to God?* If we say that money is "ours," we actually become slaves to the money. Money should be a tool in our hands for kingdom purposes. If we're not careful, money becomes a master and not a tool, and it then owns us. On the other hand, when we acknowledge that everything belongs to God, we truly serve him and money becomes an instrument for righteous purposes.

In Deuteronomy 8:17-18, we read, "You may say to yourself, 'My power and the strength of my hands have produced this wealth for me.' But remember the LORD your God, for it is he who gives you the ability to produce wealth…"

A fatal flaw in our thinking takes root when we begin believing our growing bank account is the result of our own efforts. A true humility helps us understand that it all comes from God. He gave us whatever abilities we use to earn money. This is equally true whether we work in a factory or in an office tower. Because it *does* all come from God, it is therefore vital to understand that we have stewardship responsibilities for what he places in our hands. We are not handling *our* money. We are handling *his* money and should be directing it where he instructs. Once we understand we are stewards and not owners, we can adopt some careful and responsible thoughts on Giving, Debt, and Saving.

The Gift that Keeps Giving

In his book *The Blessed Life*, Pastor Robert Morris says, "There are more than 500 verses in the Bible concerning prayer and nearly 500 verses concerning faith, but more than 2,000 verses on the subject of money and possessions."*

Wow! That's more verses than we find on the topics of prayer and prophecy.

One of the most important and oft-quoted verses in all of scripture, John 3:16, states it succinctly, "For God so loved the world that he gave his only begotten Son..." Nothing in all of literature is as profound as this one thought: *God loved and God gave.*

Jim Elliot was a missionary to Ecuador. He was portrayed in the movie, *The End of the Spear.* He made a now famous entry in his journal before he was martyred by the Auca Indians. He wrote, "He is no fool who gives what he cannot keep to gain what he cannot lose."** We can apply Elliot's insight and logic to money. The wise person is not the one who knows how to build and hoard wealth but rather the one who knows how to give it away.

Giving can encompass many areas in our lives. Giving of one's time and energy does indeed represent a generosity of spirit. However, more often than not, our hearts are truly revealed by our financial giving. Jesus told us in Matthew 6 that we should be storing up treasures in heaven rather than on earth because our hearts will be where our treasure resides. Jesus understood that our money and our hearts are inseparable. Our hearts cannot be in heaven unless we send our money there first. The only way to *lay up* treasures in heaven is to *lay them down* here on earth.

> *The only way to lay up treasures in heaven is to lay them down here on earth.*

Have you ever considered making giving a lifestyle choice? The scripture is clear. God wants giving to be second nature to us, a no-brainer; a behavior that requires no second thoughts. If you err in any direction, err on the side of generosity. Give without any strings attached and give just like Father God, the greatest giver of all. Paul quoted Jesus in Acts

---

* Morris, *The Blessed Life,* 29.

** Elliot, *Shadow of the Almighty,* 108.

20:35 when he wrote, "It is more blessed to give than to receive." Say it out loud, memorize it, meditate on it, and get it into the depths of your soul. "It is more blessed to give than receive." Giving absolutely results in rewards.

In Luke 6:38, Jesus said if we give, it will be given to us in return. The return will be "a good measure, pressed down, shaken together and running over." The formula is simple. God loves—God gives; you love—you give. You give—God loves it and gives you a return. The motive is not the return; the motive is in the giving. The return is the blessing of God. When you give, you pattern your life after God's own character of giving.

Let's take a look at three areas of Giving: Tithing, Offerings, and Alms.

God's First Requirement—Tithing

In the Bible, the word *tithe* means "tenth." To tithe, or bring in the tithe, in the Old Testament connotes the practice of giving the first tenth of one's goods, production, income, or material increase back to God through the agency of his earthly priests. It's an acknowledgement that he is the source of all material blessing. The first recorded instance of this practice is found in Genesis 14 when Abraham, upon returning from victorious battle, was met by Melchizedek, King of Salem, and also known as "Priest of God Most High." (The writer of Hebrews describes Melchizedek as an Old Testament archetype of Christ.)

Melchizidek brought out bread and wine. He pronounced a blessing upon Abraham. When Abraham, in turn, gave Melchizedek a tenth of all the spoils from his victory, according to the book of Hebrews, he was symbolically tithing to Jesus.

In the Law of Moses, God commanded a tithe of all which the ground produced and also one of every ten animals. This instruction can be found in various places in the Law including Leviticus 27, Numbers 18, as well as Deuteronomy 12, 14, and 26. There were two principal reasons for the tithe in the Law. First, it recognized that everything belongs to God and that he is the source of all material blessings. Secondly, this was the method by which the material needs of the temple and the Levitical priesthood were met.

God's attitude on the tithe is clearly revealed in the third chapter of Malachi. In verses 8-11, God rhetorically asks, "'Will a man rob God? Yet you rob me. But you ask, "How do we rob you?" God continues with the answer, "'In tithes and offerings. You are under a curse—the whole nation of you—because you are robbing me. Bring the whole tithe into the storehouse, that there may be food in my house. Test me in this,' says the Lord Almighty, 'and see if I will not throw open the floodgates of heaven and pour out so much blessing that you will not have room enough for it. I will prevent pests from devouring your crops, and the vines in your fields will not cast their fruit,' says the Lord Almighty."

Now, you might be wondering how this tithing thing applies today. I'm glad you asked! I have preached and taught the principle of tithing for over forty years. The *spirit* of tithing based on the command in the Old Testament is clearly evident in the New Testament as well. Paul tells us in 1 Timothy 5:17-18, "The elders who direct the affairs of the church well are worthy of double honor, especially those whose work is preaching and teaching. For the Scripture says, 'Do not muzzle the ox while it is treading out the grain,' and 'The worker deserves his wages.'" Paul tells us further in 1 Corinthians 9:13-14, "Don't you know that those who work in the temple get their food from the temple, and those who serve at the altar share in what is offered on the altar? In the same way, the Lord has commanded that those who preach the gospel should receive their living from the gospel."

God demands the same spirit of support for today's pastors and for the needs of the local church that he required for the priesthood and the temple in the Old Testament. God's challenge in Malachi 3 is to test him in his promise. We acknowledge through our tithe that he is the source of all our material blessings and that he meets the needs of those who lead us in our local churches. God promises to respond to our tithe by pouring out blessings that are uncontainable. Failure to tithe causes these blessings to dry up.

You may be able to generate material success for a period of time, by your own abilities, even while not tithing. However, the blessing of God won't be on your effort. You'll continually be under pressure to hold on to whatever you accumulate. How much better it is to receive material blessings from God as a result of our obedience to him without all that human stress and aggravation?

I don't believe for a moment that God asks us to tithe for his benefit. Tithing prepares us for immeasurable blessings from the throne room, and, more importantly, locks us into his divine nature. After all, Jesus, as the first fruits of God's giving, was actually God's tithe! It's no wonder we are blessed when we tithe. We're mirroring an act of God. So, the first thing I do after receiving any form of income is sit down and write my tithe check.

Tithing is not only my tenth, but is intended by God to be my *first* tenth. Checks for the mortgage, utilities, car payments, and credit cards are written after my check for God's tenth. I'm not about to rob God and thereby lose his blessing. John D. Rockefeller, the great industrialist and philanthropist, said, "I never would have been able to tithe the first million dollars I made if I had not tithed on my first salary, which was $1.50 per week."

After Tithing

It probably won't be good news for those who begrudge the tithe, but tithing is not the end of biblical giving. It's the beginning. There are two other major areas of giving we need to address. The first is *offerings*. Some call this "sowing" to make a distinction from the business term *investment* on the basis that investment is made for a monetary return. I believe, however, the term *investment* in regard to offerings is a very legitimate use of the word.

Believers are in the business of extending the kingdom of God. When we invest through our offerings into people, printing and distributing Bibles, missionary support, infrastructure such as churches, schools, and orphanages or television and radio, we really do look for, pray for, and expect a return on the investment. We are looking for souls won into the kingdom as a result of these investments, and we are looking for the kingdom of God to be extended.

Nowhere is the spirit of New Testament giving more aptly described than in 2 Corinthians 8 and 9. Paul was asking the Corinthian church to follow through on its commitment to prepare an offering for the impoverished saints in Jerusalem. He reminded them of the incredible generosity of the Macedonian churches. The people in these churches had given well beyond their poverty and abilities. The overarching theme in these chapters is a spirit of generosity despite one's circumstances. God wants our offerings to be made willingly and cheerfully, not grudgingly.

There is a powerful point in these 2 Corinthians chapters relating to tithes and offerings which is of paramount importance to New Testament believers. Paul says in 8:8-9, "I am not commanding you, but I want to test the sincerity of your love by comparing it with the earnestness of others. For you know the grace of the Lord Jesus Christ, that though he was rich, yet for your sakes he became poor, so that you through his poverty might become rich."

While the Old Testament principle of the tithe was based on a command, Paul says here that he is appealing to an even greater principle. This is the principle of giving based on the profound grace demonstrated in the life of the Lord Jesus. Jesus gave everything. He became poor, spent his life in serving, and ultimately died with absolutely no material wealth of any kind. This picture of Jesus reminds us that while in the Old Testament people gave ten percent based on a command, in the New Testament Jesus gave everything out of grace. Paul was asking them to exhibit that same spirit of Jesus in their giving. It goes right back to the essence of John 3:16: God loved and God gave.

Consider the Following Truths Found in the Word of God

- We have been born again and we have been delivered out of darkness into his kingdom.
- We have been adopted into the family of God, and we are now his sons.

- We have been set free from the power of sin.
- We have access to the throne of God.
- We have been fully justified and made righteous.
- We are sinless in his sight, and we are sealed for the day of redemption.

When we ponder the immeasurable grace of God in what has been accomplished for us, should not the tithe, the ten percent, be merely a baseline, a minimum for our giving? Are we not more greatly obligated in our giving under grace than under the Law? Under the Law, God commanded ten percent. Under grace, Jesus gave everything. How could we to give less?

Sow in Fertile Soil

Here are a few good principles for offerings. Make sure your seed is falling into good soil. Give to that which is worthy. Don't be emotionally drawn to fruitless or shallow ministries. If you're going to be a good kingdom investor, sow your resources into productive kingdom investments which demonstrably bring people out of darkness into the light. Regularly review your "Kingdom Portfolio." Jesus said the seed sown on good ground produced a crop thirty, sixty, and one hundred times the amount of seed originally sown. Look for a real, measurable kingdom return on your offerings.

Look for a real, measurable kingdom return on your offerings.

We Have an Obligation to the Poor

The third type of giving I want to discuss is known as *alms* giving. These are gifts given directly to people who are absolutely unable to repay. Jesus described alms gifts in Matthew 6 as given in secret, without the left hand knowing what the right hand is doing. Though all types of giving will return blessings, I doubt anything touches the heart of God more, or will be more personally gratifying, than giving to the poor.

God's concern for the poor permeates all of Scripture. God condemned injustices to the poor, the widows, and the fatherless. He condemned the stealing of their food, means, and property.

In Isaiah 1:23 we read, "Your rulers are rebels, companions of thieves; they all love bribes and chase after gifts. They do not defend the cause of the fatherless; the widow's case does not come before them."

In Psalm 82:2-4 we read, "How long will you defend the unjust and show partiality to the wicked? Defend the cause of the weak and fatherless; maintain the rights of the poor and oppressed. Rescue the weak and the needy; deliver them from the hand of the wicked."

Further, note that in Luke 4:18, Jesus declared the Holy Spirit was upon him because he had been anointed to preach the good news to the poor.

God is deeply and vehemently concerned for the poor. We should have the same heart. Speaking of the man who fears the Lord, we read in Psalm 112:9, "He has scattered abroad his gifts to the poor, his righteousness endures forever; his horn will be lifted high in honor." That's a pretty good return for a man who chooses to bless those who cannot provide for themselves. The horn in Scripture is a symbol of power and authority. Not only will your gifts to the poor ensure that your righteousness endures forever, but your leadership and authority in this life will be lifted high in honor. You will be esteemed by God for your compassion to the needy. God's esteem is far better than the esteem of men.

If we use our financial blessings only for our own benefit, we totally miss the heart of God. We have been blessed in order to bless others. Since we have freely received the grace of God, we are expected to freely, liberally, and generously give. It's impossible to out-give God. The more we give, the more we recognize how much abundance God has already poured out in our lives, and the more perceptive we become to all he gives in return.

Taking the Sting Out of Debt

In order to make a point regarding the scourge of debt, my mother would regularly put a spin on the words found in 1 Corinthians 15:55 which reads, "O death, where is thy sting?" (KJV). To be sure, there is also plenty of "sting" in debt. The only difference between death and debt is that while *death* is terminal, *debt* causes an interminable death.

Men, as heads of families, it is crucial that you take a good, hard look at debt. There is not a more debt-driven society on the planet than our own here in America. Christians are, sadly, not immune to the pervasiveness of personal debt. It destroys marriages and families routinely and has driven many to suicide.

I want to be very strong here on my position about debt. Earlier in this chapter I discussed the "mammon" spirit. When we think we own the money, it actually owns us. Especially with monetary debt, this false notion of our own control is most deadly. Debt proceeds directly out of the "mammon" system and is not a program created by God. Debt is the ultimate slave-master and ultimately a real killer. Debt has no remorse and no pity. Jesus told us Satan comes only to steal, kill, and destroy. Satan will use all his deceptions and tricks to entice us into debt. His endgame is our total destruction. Proverbs 22:7 says, "Just as the rich rule the poor, so the borrower is servant to the lender" (NLT).

Our economy in America today is based on 20% production of goods and 80% on the offering of services. One of the largest service industries, if not the largest, is banking. The vast majority of profits earned by the largest banks in America is earned on credit card debt. Without the interest and fees earned on credit cards, these large banks would be in real trouble, and their shareholders would be very unhappy. No wonder banks have spent many years and many dollars making it easy for many of us to pile up stacks of plastic. The bigger our stacks, the more likely we are to also pile up stacks of high-interest debt.

Even folks who have gone through personal bankruptcy will eventually receive new offers for credit cards—with high interest rates and fees "necessary" to re-establish credit.

We must recognize the credit card and other debt industries for what they are! The whole spirit of this system is predatory. We must be vigilant here for ourselves and those who rely on us. Credit card debts keep us in bondage.

Let's face it. Let's say it like it is. We go into debt for *stuff*. It's mostly stuff we *want* rather than stuff we *need*. I'm convinced, for most of the stuff we buy on credit, we rarely ever ask God's opinion on whether or not we should buy the stuff in the first place. In fact, I think we are generally embarrassed to come to God and ask him his thoughts on buying that five-thousand dollar plasma screen TV on credit because we already know what he would say.

The world tries daily to seduce us into buying stuff. If we respond to the advertising and other persuasion, we leverage ourselves to the max and get locked up in a metaphorical debtor's prison. We mortgage our future. We play right into the hands of the enemy! Once in debt for "junk," we can't make kingdom investments with "fruit that remains." Under a load of debt, we enjoy no peace in our lives and are constantly under emotional pressure to manage it all. Cracks begin to form in our marriages and home life and these spidery cracks of stress and financial anxiety run out to all other activities—our family activities, church involvement, and our jobs.

I'm not going to soft peddle this with some statement like, "I know we all need houses, cars, clothes and food." Of course we do. In Matthew 6, Jesus said the Father knows we need these things.

Please understand that you're my beloved brethren, and I passionately want to protect you from the horror of debt. We must ask what we believe. Can God provide for me, or do I need to be enslaved by the mammon system for my well-being? By being enslaved in debt, I am buying into the subtle satanic suggestion that God can't or won't provide for me. It's a Garden of Eden experience all over again, "Has God really said?" Did Jesus really mean it when he said if I would seek first the kingdom and his righteousness, all these things would be provided for me?

Have your heard these phrases whispered in your ear? "You need credit cards to establish credit." "God wants you to be blessed." "It's on sale." "For just a little more per month, you can have the top model." And, so forth. It's not a matter of owning a house, but the biggest house. It's not simply a car, but the top model or one of those fancy, foreign jobs. It's not just a suit, but a designer suit. It's just a lot of stuff we don't really need.

You might have heard that with debt, you'll have "credit power." The ability to buy stuff on credit provides a false sense of wealth, success, and well-being. Satan, through the mammon system, wants to watch us slowly sink in the quicksand and smother. It's not "credit power," it's "debt power," and those controlled by it go directly to our culture's version of debtor's prison and do not pass "Go."

Now, here's the bottom line. If you have to go into debt for a bunch of stuff, you don't really need the stuff. If, however, you meet your giving obligations, make your house and car payments on time, put food on the table and clothes on the kid's backs, put some money in savings and have cash left over, then feel free to buy the better suit. With this thinking and these priorities, let me offer a little hard-earned advice.

> *If you have to go into debt for a bunch of stuff, you don't really need the stuff.*

Saving and Investing

In Proverbs 1:3, Solomon tells us his sayings were written down for the purpose of "acquiring a disciplined and prudent life." Money management, especially saving money, should be done with prudence and discipline. It takes discipline to say no to the temptations of debt and yes to putting some money away.

Debt goes on the books because we want stuff immediately. Like a child, we want something *now*. A child's perspective is no way to manage finances. Would you give a child your debit card? We naturally intuit that saving money takes hard work and true grit. It requires looking out further in time and quelling the urge to run down to the mall and buy more trinkets. In our fast food, instant gratification world, this is really tough on our flesh. We like the smell of new leather in a new car, not to mention that fancy GPS system. There are a lot of new technologies, gadgets, and gizmos being marketed. The price tag can be very high, and when you drive that new car off the lot, it's suddenly worth a lot less, and you'll be thinking soon about the next new vehicle. Guys, it's foolish to allow ourselves to fall into that trap!

The Book of Proverbs is replete with financial advice and wisdom. In 13:11 Solomon says, "Dishonest money dwindles away, but he who gathers money little by little makes it grow."

In order to build wealth, we need to really take the long look. Winning the lottery or making a quick buck on a stock tip teaches us nothing about stewardship. But we learn as we build little by little. So be very cautious before putting money into any quick-buck or get-rich-quick scheme. This kind of investing is usually just gambling; and we all know Las Vegas is built on the backs of gamblers who convince themselves that they can be the exception to the general rule that, sooner or later, the casino wins.

The alternative to playing for an easy win against the odds is to work in God's way, to be made into a Teleios Man. Proverbs 21:5 says, "The plans of the diligent lead to profit as surely as haste leads to poverty." Saving money takes diligence. Saving money develops real discipline and perseverance. James tells us "perseverance must finish its work" so we may be "mature and complete" lacking nothing in our character (1:4). "Mature and complete." *Teleios!*

I personally cannot think of a bigger character builder than saving money. I'll say it again, because I feel so strongly about this warning. Debt enslaves us and renders us incapable of kingdom influence in the world. Saving sets us free and gives us many options and opportunities.

Oh, by the way, our savings belong to God too. He may, from time to time, ask us to go into our savings to meet someone's need. If and when he does, our positive response will always be an act of obedience and a step of faith—both signs of our spiritual development, our "completion in Christ."

Jesus told a parable in Matthew 25 and Luke 19 about the servants to whom a master gave certain sums of money. Time passed and, upon his return, the master asked for an accounting of the money. One of the servants had done nothing with what he'd been given. The master rebuked the servant, telling him he should have at least banked the money and earned some interest. Some will suggest this parable has only "spiritual" application and is not really speaking about handling hard money.

Jesus used the example because it represents a valid, real-life picture of a master's expectation. Our Master rightfully expects a return from the resources he places in our hands, including financial resources.

In this parable, Jesus teaches us about savings and investment. He warns us that mishandling financial resources can incur the displeasure of the master. We simply aren't following Scripture or being spiritual if we don't build savings or invest wisely. It's not necessary to start saving large amounts in the beginning, but it's necessary to start! Put a little away each month, and the Lord will add his blessing and your character will broaden and deepen.

David Livingstone, the famous Scottish missionary and explorer in Africa, is quoted as saying, "I will place no value on anything I have or possess except in relation to the kingdom of Christ. If anything I have will advance that kingdom, it shall be given or kept whichever will best promote the glory of him to whom I owe all my hopes, both for time and eternity." What an awesome and balanced view of handling the Lord's resources! Giving and saving extend the kingdom of God through proper spiritual management of the resources God has placed in our hands.

Long-Term Investing

First, we learn how to get out of debt, and how to give, and how to save. Then, we take a look at wise investing.

My long-time friend Michael Papson has been a very successful financial planner for many years. When we teach men at our Mentoring Intensives, I always ask Michael to speak. I've asked Michael to give us an overview of his thoughts about investing based on his successes in over twenty years in the financial services industry.

Cornerstone Concepts

First of all, personal money management is unique to each individual's financial goals and dreams. That's why my first suggestion is to have a credentialed financial coach/advisor with whom you can develop a trusting, long-term relationship. That individual should be able to help you do the following:

- Set goals for buying a home, educating your children, retirement, etc.
- Determine how much you will need in order to meet these goals
- Prepare for the unforeseen—i.e., premature death, disability, etc.
- Determine what resources are available to invest for these objectives
- Set up a diversified investment plan
- Monitor your progress
- Review and update your objectives as necessary

Frankly, a financial advisor's most valuable role is to protect the client against his or her own behavior which often can be impetuous or undisciplined. Over the long term, "wealth accumulation" is determined not as much by investment performance but by investor behavior. Most people invariably make emotional mistakes when it comes to money and investing, particularly in times of inflation and precipitous market shifts.

Here are the key areas where a qualified financial advisor can provide assistance:

- **Financial Position**—Monitoring resources you have available to attain your financial goals
- **Reserve Strategies**—Managing your cash for emergencies and opportunities

- **Protection Planning**—Ensuring that your most valuable assets are adequately protected against loss
- **Tax Planning**—Helping to minimize the impact of taxes on your portfolio and income both while you are working and later during retirement
- **Education Planning**—Saving and planning appropriately to allow loved ones to attend the college they choose and deserve
- **Retirement Planning**—Reaching "financial independence" (when work is optional and retirement affordable)
- **Estate Planning**—Making sure your assets are passed most efficiently to whomever you choose without undue reduction for taxes and administrative costs

Another key principle in planning and investing involves determining your "investment philosophy." Each person views his or her life, and therefore financial world, differently. A step in understanding an individual's investment philosophy is by assessing one's risk tolerance, a concept which could fill ten more pages. However, a simple way to do this assessment is to answer questions on a risk tolerance quiz, such as those easily found doing a "Google" search for "Risk Tolerance." Here's one such site: http://www.rcre.rutgers.edu/money/riskquiz/.

Investment philosophy also requires a macro view of characterizing your assets. I would call this the "four cornerstone philosophy." Or think of a stool supported by four legs.

Cornerstone One: Cash Reserves—this would be money saved in a checking account, money market account, or savings account for emergency or opportunity reasons.

Cornerstone Two: Insurance/Protection—this involves having the correct amount of life insurance, disability insurance, homeowner's insurance, long-term care insurance, etc., depending on where you are in life and what you are trying to protect. For example, what good is starting an investment program to save for retirement or for your child's education if you suffer an unexpected disability—or worse, death—which eliminates your savings, curtails your income, and throws your family into a crisis? You can and should plan for life's contingencies. "In this world you will have trouble" (John 16:33).

After the first two cornerstones are adequately addressed, then you are ready to proceed to cornerstones three and four. Unless you've already established adequate cash reserves and asset protection, pass up those "hot" stock tips of Uncle Joe's!

Cornerstone Three: Fixed Investments—these types of investments provide a consistent rate of return and provide stability to your portfolio. Also, they provide peace of mind for those times of anticipated financial need, such as income during retirement. Examples of fixed investments are certificates of deposits, fixed annuities, government and corporate bonds.

Cornerstone Four: Equity Investments—when your goals require you to significantly increase your assets over the long term (five years or more), equity investments can offer the growth you're looking for. Examples of equity assets are: stocks, growth mutual funds, real estate, variable annuities, and commodities.

Having a qualified financial advisor working with you enhances the probability that the above cornerstones will be effectively and properly implemented. We all could use a coach in most areas. Drew Brees is a great football player, but he doesn't expect to win without a coach to focus his talent and teammates to capitalize on his talent, all in an environment of mutual encouragement, clear-headed analysis, and professional accountability.

Why is Good Advice Important?

The fact is, most Americans will never meet their goals. I'll go one step further—most Americans never brainstorm their goals and end up with a recipe for one or more of these:

1. No discipline in their finances
2. Lack of defined financial goals
3. Inappropriate investment selection/diversification
4. Poor money management
5. No annual spending and saving plan
6. Accumulation of consumer debt

The bottom line? "Those that fail to plan are planning to fail."

I appreciate Michael, and I'm grateful that he was willing to share his sage advice. I wish I had known him when I was newly married. I could have used this information at that most critical time. Rather, early on, I broke just about every one of the rules recommended here.

Earlier in the chapter I mentioned the book *The Blessed Life* by Robert Morris. I have never seen, read, or heard anything relating to money that was as transformational as this book. Do yourself a favor and order one today. You can purchase it online at www.gatewaypeople.com.

I want to leave you with one last scripture. In *The Message* version of Philippians 4:19, Eugene Peterson says, "You can be sure that God will take care of everything you need, his generosity exceeding even yours in the glory that pours from Jesus."

I want you to memorize this scripture and rest in it. Regardless of how many financial mistakes you've made in the past, God wants you to know that he has you covered. Failures in your past need not destroy your future. By learning well from them, they can make possible any future successes.

Chapter 10

Your Personality

WE ARE EACH ONE OF A KIND, THANK GOD!

M Y DAUGHTER TRINA HAS been bringing great delight to me over the course of her life. She's a fun-loving, life-of-the-party, bounce-off-the-walls poster child for the sanguine personality (more on this terminology later). I'll ratchet that up a notch and says she's "sanguine-on-steroids."

Trina is an ultra people-oriented person. She loves being the star of the show, operates from an inexhaustible reserve of energy, and has an insatiable desire for fun. She talks to everyone and everyone loves talking to her. If you know her, you'll be smiling and nodding agreement. That's Trina.

When Trina goes to a party, she's just convinced everyone came to see her. She's in her element with people, and the more the merrier. It doesn't really matter who is there as long as there's a crowd! She's not only the life of the party, but if there's no party to go to, she'll throw one herself. She loves to entertain and brings everyone within a hundred-mile radius into her fun. Her house is filled with people at all times, especially young people. They think she's one of them. The truth is—she is!

She loves her kids and everyone else's kids. Little babies stop crying as soon as she holds them. Her New Year's resolution is always the same, "Let's have fun this year!"

On the other hand, my son, Aaron, is an intellectual good ol' boy. He's laid back, rarely gets anxious, and is never in a hurry. It's unlikely he'll ever have a heart attack or nervous breakdown because his pulse never rises, and I don't think he has any nerves. Everyone likes him, and he likes everyone. He has incredible patience and is very compassionate. When growing up, Aaron was totally himself and was completely impervious to peer pressure. He has deep and unmovable convictions. Of course, that could be said of anyone in our family.

Aaron is content, not demanding, and is willing to let others take the lead. His university students love his classes because he makes physics and astronomy understandable and fun. His perfect day is doing nothing, watching a basketball game, and taking a long nap. Aaron exemplifies about two-thirds of all men—just good ol' boys whom everyone likes. The ancient Greek word that describes his personality is *phlegmatic*.

My wife, Devi, is the vivacious *choleric* personality in our family. She is very determined, decisive, purpose-driven, and visionary. In terms of corporate leadership, she's a CEO. Devi also has a lot of *sanguine* traits that make her confident personality even more outgoing. (Could someone pass me the Valium?)

Devi is animated when talking on the phone. When she's talking to me in bed, with the room darkened, I can vaguely see her arms flailing in the air as if someone could see her gestures. Everything she does is extravagant.

If Devi could have been in the boat with the disciples, instead of walking on the water like Simon Peter, she would have jumped out with great fanfare and run to Jesus. Anyone within earshot would have heard her suggestion to Jesus that he might want to consider meeting her half way. She would have cast a questioning gaze back to the diffident disciples, wondering why they weren't following her. I imagine her yelling at the disciples, "Come on, let's go! What are you waiting for? Jesus is out here!" By force of personality, she would have compelled them to go with her. Then Devi would have finished off her water running experience with a social event. "I know what we can do! Let's all go to that lovely

Galilean fresh seafood restaurant before we return to Capernaum—you know, the one that has white linen tablecloths and napkins."

Phew! I'm exhausted just thinking about it.

Then There's Me

Then there's me. I tend to be methodical and introspective—a real perfectionist. At times I can be somewhat negative and moody. I hate to admit it, but I can be a little slow, stubborn, and defensive. If I'm not careful, it's possible for me to get in the kind of negative mind-set which says, "You think I've got a problem? You've just identified who the real problem is—it's *you*, pal!" My feelings can be hurt easily at times.

I've been known to be a bit paranoid about my health and my family's safety too. If I catch a cold, it's probably turning into cancer. If you're late coming home, I can just visualize the car wreck. I'm sometimes tempted to not pursue my goals because I'm "sure" they'll fail.

I can be picky and controlling about other things as well. Whatever the amount of my paycheck, it isn't enough. We'll probably run out of grocery money and die before the month is over. I like nice things, and I don't like ugly things. I move and think impulsively then count the cost later. Every hair is in place, or I'll pull it out. My toothpaste is squeezed only from the end, and God forbid that you or anyone else, including Devi, should squeeze it from the middle. And, no, I never let anyone borrow my toothpaste.

My socks match exactly, my shoes are polished, and my shirts are starched. I don't like making mistakes, and I can spot them in others a mile away. I like my world to be perfect, so please don't mess it up. I have the "gift" of criticism. I'm right about everything, and I'm very, very inflexible.

When we take vacations, we must begin at 6:00 a.m. sharp. If you're late, I'll leave you. Your suitcases must be packed and sitting by the car by 5:45 or they stay home with you. We're going to have fun between 2:00 and 5:00 p.m. We will have dinner at 6:00 p.m. and be in bed by 9:00. The family bus won't stop for potty breaks until we've driven four hours or until bladders rupture, whichever comes first. Of course, I believe in divine healing, so I'll pray for your bladder while I keep driving. After all, this is a vacation, and if you're going to ride along with me, you'd better pack your sense of humor. You should also pack your own toothpaste.

I exaggerate a bit to make a point, but I really do show this behavior associated with the *melancholic*. More positively portrayed, a melancholic person shows attention to detail, has high standards, and is creative as well as conscientious and self-sacrificing. These *beneficial* behaviors of the melancholic are often associated with the choleric (Devi) personality. Yet, they are frequently eclipsed in the melancholic by a perfectionist mentality. A perfectionist can concentrate on his weaknesses rather than building upon his strengths and thereby paralyze himself.

The Has-Beens!

I've described my family's temperaments and invaded their privacy for a couple of reasons. Oh, they've come to expect this from me, so not to worry. First, I want you to know them. Secondly, each one of us represents an excellent example of the four distinct personality types or temperaments, commonly known as *sanguine*, *phlegmatic*, *choleric*, and *melancholic*.

...the four distinct personality types or temperaments, commonly known as sanguine, phlegmatic, choleric, and melancholic.

Much of what used to be true of me is now securely in the "Has-Been" file. I've changed. (Really!) Those characteristics no longer describe my behavior. Here's the trick. *If a person is open and honest about his personality weaknesses, he can turn them into strengths.* I tell you, men, do not be afraid to look in the mirror and honestly see yourself! Do this: establish a baseline personality inventory of yourself, and you're on the starting line for an improvement run. Don't forget, you have to start with an honest self-appraisal.

After learning about these personality types, I was able to make solid progress in my own behaviors. Until that time, I fretted more about containing my weaknesses than I did trying to release my strengths.

You can do the same. I'm excited just thinking about handing you a new tool. I am absolutely convinced I can help you with this. The subject is worth many books, but I'm going to summarize by hitting the high points here. Read on!

Melancholy personalities are more prone to depression than others because we are the most creative and introspective. As I've related in Chapter 2, I've had my share of depression, and to this day I must guard against it. Anxiety over money, fear of an uncertain future (which is really a lack of trust in God's plan for my life), and a tendency toward negativism are some of my own hurdles. I talk out the money anxiety with Devi since she has more than enough confidence in the financial area. The uncertain future? I talk out with God and do a lot of praying in the Spirit. I take care of negativism by refusing to speak words that are negative. Occasionally all three of these worries can lie in wait and try to bushwhack me, like a scene out of an old cowboy movie. So, I keep my ear to the ground and am aware of conditions and circumstances that might predispose me to depression. The key is awareness.

Each temperament has both strengths and weaknesses. If you are strength-led, you will be powerful in God's kingdom. If you are led by your weaknesses, you are not likely to flourish and get God's full blessing for your life. The good news is you can bring improvement to your personality without doing injury to your nature.

Guys, you must first understand and then appreciate your own personality. You have to value yourself, since God made you. When we learn that we are "fearfully and wonderfully made" (Ps. 139:14), we can embrace the unique, purposeful, and glorious design given us by the Creator!

It is critical that you understand your own personality and your corresponding strengths and weakness. You'll grow spiritually and emotionally. You'll also have a better understanding of others.

Other Benefits of Temperament Awareness

Unexpected blessings appear as you embrace your own unique temperament and the temperaments of others. For example, you'll value diversity in others. This is especially important when it comes to your wife and children. Instead of being irritated by certain idiosyncrasies and mannerisms, you learn to appreciate them. You begin to see them as God created them to be. You'll be less likely to try changing them to fit your preconceptions. You won't be as inclined to being judgmental or critical.

Understanding the temperaments of others will enhance your communication skills. Your approach to others will be calibrated by an understanding of what turns them on or off. Coaching, teaching, and supporting are all more effectively done as you understand others as they have been made.

Fathers, take the time to understand the diversity of your kids' personalities. When Trina was a child, I would make her go to her room to study. We didn't know at the time how counterproductive this was, since we had not learned about the temperaments. Being sent to her room to study seemed like punishment to Trina. Our sanguine daughter couldn't study in that environment. There weren't any people there! She wanted lots of noise, loud music, and interaction with people! Conversely, Aaron's personality required the solitude of a monk and an atmosphere of peace and calm before he could really study. His room was a sanctuary in which he could focus. Being there wasn't a punishment!

If a leader understands temperaments, he can make wise decisions when it comes to job assignments. Putting a person in the wrong position sets that person up for failure. Placing a person in the right place stages them for success.

A choleric, for example, always needs to lead and will most likely be unhappy and frustrated as only a follower. A sanguine saint doesn't enjoy working alone, and a melancholic brother is not happy in an environment of confusion and disorder. The phlegmatic personality can be counted on to be loyal but might not be the best choice for an administrative position.

A lot of good books have been written in the past three decades on these personality traits. Most of the authors replace the ancient Greek names with colors, animals, acronyms, biblical characters, or other descriptors. Essentially these new labels mean the same thing. So, for the sake of simplicity, I'll use the ancient Greek terms *choleric, sanguine, phlegmatic* and *melancholic*. Besides, my name Titus is Greek, so I have a certain fondness for Greek terms.

My Introduction to the Temperaments

Devi first read a book on personality traits. She finished the last page, slammed the book shut, and excitedly announced, "Honey, you've got to read this book! You can fill out a personality profile and it will help you understand yourself."

"I don't believe in all that psychobabble," I replied. I'd grown weary of the self-help genre.

"Ironically," she said, "that's exactly what the book predicts a melancholic person will say when asked to fill out a personality profile."

She got me. Devi's choleric/sanguine personality makes her a teacher by nature. As soon as she learns something, she wants to share it with others. And, of course, since I was in proximity, I was her first student. I was in the cross-hairs, and she is an expert truth-sharpshooter, so there was no escape.

Oh no, not again! I thought. *My toxic gut syndrome was last month, and the spiritual gifts test was the month before that. I just finished eating spinach because of my runaway pituitary. I still don't understand if my colors are Fall, Spring, Winter, or Summer. On top of everything else, I have to do this personality thing?*

I knew resistance was futile. When Devi gets an idea, it's as though the Hounds of Heaven are turned loose. I heard them barking, and I knew they were coming my way. I sighed and took the personality profile. It hit the bull's eye. It described me perfectly.

Please Welcome Mike Weiher!

Mike Weiher teaches personalities and mannerisms for our Men's Intensives. Because Mike is such a gifted teacher and does such an excellent job unfolding the patterns of personalities to men, I wanted him to share some of these truths with you.

Mike Weiher's Guide to Appreciating God's Original Design In Ourselves and Others

In recent years, I have spent a lot of time studying personality types. I have come to deeply appreciate the unique traits and mannerisms which God gives us. God not only crafted my personality and said, "It is very good," but he also enjoys my temperament—he likes me! Just as important, I can now better understand and relate to other people through an assessment of their individual styles.

Let me make a strong disclaimer. I am not talking here about the study of worldly psychology! I'm using the truths of human nature found in the Bible. Thus, this understanding of mannerisms and types does not come from Freud or other psychological theorists.

The Origin of Personality Description

The four basic mannerism styles were first observed by the ancient Greek Hippocrates about four hundred years before the birth of Jesus. He recognized four distinct personality types and gave them the following names: the choleric, the sanguine, the phlegmatic, and the melancholic. These names were a result of his belief that one's mannerisms were attributable to four fluids in the body, namely yellow bile, blood, phlegm, and black bile. We don't associate bodily fluids any more with these personality types, but the four basic classifications and their names have survived to this day.

There are many books out there that provide in-depth understanding about personalities or temperaments. In the limited space I have here, I want to summarize these types by giving you fictitious examples.

The Confident Choleric

Choleric Chris is dominant, direct, and makes decisions quickly. He is bold, determined, optimistic—a born leader. He has the ability to see the big picture and gives sensible direction as a leader. He wants summarized reports from his staff without a lot of detail. He is goal-oriented and has many friends. Company CEOs are often choleric. He motivates people to action, is comfortable delegating responsibility, and his motto is, "Do it my way, now!" Only about 3% of the population has choleric mannerisms.[*]

The Enthusiastic Sanguine

Sanguine Steve is influential, interactive, and inspirational. He is outgoing, spontaneous, and talkative. He enjoys being around a group of people even if they are strangers. He loves to tell stories to any willing listeners. He agrees with Shakespeare that "All the world is a stage." He is energetic and loves to persuade people. His positive outlook, charming mannerisms, and great sense of humor enable him to make friends easily. He is people-oriented, and his motto is "Let's have fun!" About 11% of men have sanguine mannerisms.

The Easygoing Phlegmatic

Phlegmatic Phil is steady, sensible, and not easily upset. He is pleasant, content, patient, and agreeable. He tends to be organized, relatively unemotional, gentle, and sympathetic. He is quiet but can be witty with a "dry" sense of humor. He is a good listener, develops close friends, is loyal, values family and is people oriented. He is balanced, competent, effective under pressure, and finds the simplest way to do things. He is peacemaking, and his motto is, "Easy does it!" The phlegmatic is by far the most common type; about 69% of the population is in this category.

---

[*] The percentages noted in this section are from Sandy Kulkin and The Institute for Motivational Living (800-779-3472).

The Creative Melancholic

Melancholy Michael is creative, correct, and conscientious. He is talented, idealistic, and often artistically or musically gifted. His mannerisms are serious, analytical, detailed, and accurate. He is schedule-directed, hard-working, self-sacrificing, and goal-oriented. He is often very intelligent but doesn't enjoy being the center of attention. He is cautious and careful and doesn't make friends quickly. He sets high standards for himself and others, follows the rules, and his motto is "Do the job right!" About 17% of men have melancholy mannerisms.

At the Restaurant

To illustrate each mannerism style, let's take Chris, Steve, Michael, and Phil to a restaurant and observe their behavior.

Choleric Chris not only chose the table where we would eat but also instructed each of us where to sit. He had already glanced at the menu and made his choice before the waitress arrived. He led the waitress through the ordering process, concisely instructing her about his choice of drink and meal as well as when to bring the check. He directed our conversation throughout the meal, keeping us on point.

Sanguine Steve was very happy for my invitation saying, "Oh, this will be fun!" As we waited to be seated, he had us smiling with his stories. He was dressed in bright clothes and walked confidently, smiling at everyone who looked his way. The waitress arrived, but he hadn't looked at the menu due to his non-stop conversation. He apologized charmingly and asked for a few more minutes to make his decision. When it was time to pay the tab, he reached for his wallet and realized he'd forgotten to bring it!

Phlegmatic Phil was glad to hear that we were going to the same restaurant that he and his family frequented. When the waitress arrived, she asked if he would be having his usual. He gave a shy grin and nodded. Although he was quiet during much of the meal, his humorous one-liners had us laughing. The little talking he did centered on our families and his. Thanks to his presence, we all enjoyed a peaceful meal.

Melancholic Michael seemed a little reluctant to answer my invitation, saying he'd have to check his calendar. When I asked him where he would like to go, he gave me a rather detailed run-down of the best and worst restaurants in the area. Before making a decision about his order, he carefully read through the entire menu. He had several detailed questions for the waitress concerning his order. He asked for several lemon slices with his water, butter rather than margarine, and a complete run down of the dressing and dessert choices.

Appreciate God's Originality in You

"For you created my inmost being; you knit me together in my mother's womb. I praise you because I am fearfully and wonderfully made; your works are wonderful, I know that full well. My frame was not hidden from you when I was made in the secret place. When I was woven together in the depths of the earth, your eyes saw my unformed body. All the days ordained for me were written in your book before one of them came to be" (Ps. 139:13-16).

God created each of us to be unique, one-of-a-kind masterpieces. He intends for us to fulfill a special function in the body of Christ. He sees us as priceless treasures with an essential purpose in his eternal plan.

Stop reading now and begin to thank God for ...

- Your personality or mannerism style.
- The unique way he made you.
- No mistakes were made when you were created!
- He sees you as a priceless treasure.
- He has a beautiful purpose for your life.

Self-Appreciation is a Bold First Step

Perhaps you recognize yourself in one or two of these descriptions (most of us are a blend of two types). Remember, you are highly valued by God, and he meant for you to have your personality. Learn to accept yourself as God made you and celebrate the awesome man he designed. He desires for you to live by your strengths and not to excuse your weaknesses saying, "Oh well, that's just the way I am," or "I can't help the way God made me!"

Don't believe the lies of the enemy when he says, "You've always been like this. You'll never change. God can't use you!" Declare the truth that, "He who began a good work in you will carry it on to completion until the day of Christ Jesus" (Phil. 1:6).

He will enable you to change from a person dominated by weakness to one who walks in the strengths of his God-given personality.

Appreciate God's Diversity in Others

Have you ever thought, *Why does that person act the way he does?* Maybe you've been confused thinking, *Why do Christians fail so often in their relationships?* Many of our relationship problems result from misunderstandings about each other's mannerisms and personality types.

The first step toward improving our relationships is a determination to ask, "What makes that person tick?" As we commit to developing an understanding of other peoples' personality styles, we gain great insight from the Lord about how to relate to them. Start your study of mannerisms with the most important people in your life—your wife and children.

Movement and Motivation

People operate at different speeds. People have different goals and intentions that show through their actions and behaviors. You can probably think of people close to you that move so much faster (or slower) than you do. You may also recognize that some people tend to center their lives around people while others emphasize task completion or attaining goals.

The choleric personality tends to make decisions rapidly. He moves quickly and relentlessly toward his highest priorities, which are his goals. A sanguine is similar to the choleric since he is energetic and fast moving. However, the sanguine is concerned with people while the choleric is driven to complete tasks and achieve goals.

The phlegmatic is strongly motivated by relationships. However, the phlegmatic is not spontaneous and makes deliberate decisions. He moves relatively slowly. Similarly, the melancholic's mannerisms tend to be cautious and premeditated. However, he resembles the choleric in his emphasis on achievement rather than on relationships.

We can illustrate this with a simple diagram.

Behavior	Motivated by people	Motivated by tasks
Fast-moving	Choleric	Sanguine
Deliberately-moving	Melancholy	Phlegmatic

How Each Style Is Refreshed

The personality types rejuvenate or recover energy in different ways. Have you ever noticed how family vacations can be a disaster? The choleric refreshes with physical activity, the sanguine with social interaction, the phlegmatic by relaxing and doing nothing, and the melancholic refreshes by being alone. Families might have discordance as they try to refresh using a common activity that doesn't actually refresh everyone.

The diagram below shows how mannerism styles diagonal from each other are also in direct opposition to each other. In a marriage relationship where opposites have attracted and then married each other, there is a need to reconcile methods of refreshment!

Personality Types Chosen Refreshment Activity	
Choleric Physical Activity	**Sanguine** Social Interaction
Melancholic Being Alone	**Phlegmatic** Doing Nothing

Remember the words of Jesus in Matthew 20:26-28: "Whoever wants to become great among you must be your servant, and whoever wants to be first must be your slave—just as the Son of Man did not come to be served, but to serve, and to give his life as a ransom for many." We must prefer each other and serve each other by providing opportunity for refreshment.

What Do the Personality Types Fear?

Do you want to know how to avoid pushing the wrong button in each of these personality styles? The greatest fear of the choleric is that others will take advantage of him. For the sanguine, it is the fear of rejection or loss of social approval. The phlegmatic most fears change or a loss of security. A melancholic person fears criticism.

God wants you to impact others with his love through your mannerism style. It is no secret that the cry of every human heart is to experience peaceful and loving relationships. Take an active role in building harmony and love into your relationships! As you learn to understand and appreciate the God-given personalities of others, you will also learn how to adjust your communication and approach to them.

Use Relationship Skills in Marriage

If you think on these things, your marriage will be richer. Remember men (those of us who have found our help-meets), when you met, you were attracted to your wife's traits. However, some characteristics that drew you to her before you were married can become sources of irritation after you are married. The first step is an attitude of acceptance. Be positive about your wife in your thought life. What we keep in our minds affects our speech and actions.

Your Choleric Wife. Focus on the positive. Do not be intimidated by her natural tendency to lead.

Your Sanguine Wife. Accept her lack of attention to detail. Allow for her need for spontaneity, excitement, and variety.

Your Phlegmatic Wife. Patiently accept her tendency to move slower when making decisions. Understand that she likes a predictable, secure, and peaceful environment.

Your Melancholic Wife. Appreciate her need to know all the facts before making a decision. Do not be affected by her disapproving or questioning facial expressions.

Words that Build. Practice using these building phrases so you can weave them into conversations when you talk with anyone.

The Choleric Personality

- You like responsibility.
- You are self-motivated.
- You can make decisions quickly.
- You meet new challenges head on.
- You can act boldly and courageously.

The Sanguine Personality

- You are charming and enjoyable.
- You are fun to be with.
- You are friendly and outgoing.

- You have the ability to express yourself well.
- You have a very positive influence on others.

The Phlegmatic Personality

- You are a very loyal person.
- You possess high family values.
- You bring calm to stressful situations.
- You are able to see both sides of a situation.
- You feel other people's pain.

The Melancholic Personality

- You are gifted and talented.
- You are very precise and accurate.
- You like to do the job right or not at all.
- You enjoy one-on-one relationships rather than large group interaction.
- You like to know all the facts before making a decision.

How to Act Around the Different Types

We can establish more rapport and "synch" faster with people by first determining their personality type then using optimal non-verbal communication.

With the Choleric Personality

- Pick up your pace if you generally tend to be more deliberate.
- Be concise and to the point when communicating.
- Follow through with your commitments. Do what you say you will do.

With the Sanguine Personality
- Listen enthusiastically to their stories
- Be complimentary about their appearance and social, relational impact.
- Give them lots of praise and positive attention.

With the Phlegmatic Personality
- Be open and appropriately self-disclosing.
- Slow your pace; speak softly and kindly. Actively listen and show your interest.
- Avoid being demanding or overly confrontational with your kindhearted phlegmatic.

With the Melancholic Personality
- Slow your pace. Respect the melancholic's need for detailed analysis.
- Give lots of praise since this type is very self-critical.
- Avoid too much spontaneity. Be scheduled and structured.

It's probably obvious now why I wanted Mike Weiher to write the last portion of this chapter. His descriptions of personality traits are very clear and understandable. We've consistently found his training to be insightful and liberating. You can apply these truths immediately to yourself, your family, and your colleagues at work. Your fellowship with believers will be more intimate and authentic.

Start seeing people in fresh ways and with better understanding.

Men, use this teaching! Start seeing people in fresh ways and with better understanding. As you look through this new lens, you will find it easier to think and convey a genuine appreciation for those around you. I can't guarantee your observations will change them, but I can promise that it will change you!

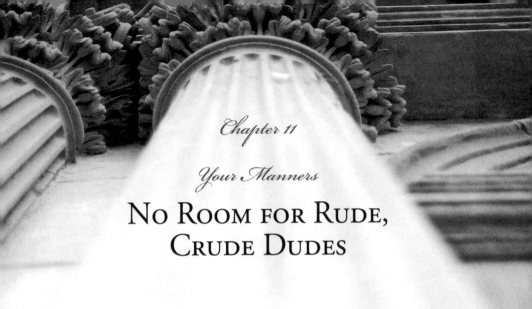

Chapter 11

Your Manners

No Room for Rude, Crude Dudes

I WAS PREPARING TO SPEAK at a men's conference in Central Ohio when a young man I'd recently met asked if he could accompany me and my assistant, Scott Sailer, on the trip. I'd met Gary earlier while speaking at a church dedication and felt it would be a good time to get to know him. I invited him along. These are great opportunities to invest in young lives.

On our way to the conference, we stopped at a steak restaurant near the retreat center. Our meal arrived, and we prayed over the food. As I opened my eyes, I looked up just in time to see Gary stab his steak and haul the entire slab up to his mouth. I was in shock. Before I realized what I was saying, I blurted out, "What are you doing?!"

"What?" he asked, shocked at my intensity.

"Your steak…" I said. I was flabbergasted.

"What about it?" Gary said.

"Your steak," I repeated. "You're lifting the whole steak up to your mouth!" I couldn't believe what I was seeing. "Put it back on your plate and cut it one bite at a time."

Then I was ashamed that I had embarrassed him. I shouldn't have reacted so quickly and sharply. I'd spoken more from reflex than reflection.

Ed Cole once made a phenomenal statement that I have never forgotten. "You should never expect someone to act in a certain way if you haven't taught them." How would Gary know that steaks shouldn't be consumed like a hotdog on a stick if no one had taught him? Recalling what I knew of his background, I realized he'd never had training in etiquette. With Ed's statement on my heart and mind, and now with the compassion of a father, I began teaching Gary about proper table manners. How could he have known?

Several years ago, Devi realized a twenty-year dream of conducting mentoring intensives for women by opening the Mentoring Mansion in Youngstown, Ohio. Devi holds training sessions for women during extended weekends and shows them creative home management and vital relationship skills. These women leave with tools which help them restore the dignity and sanctity of their homes. Importantly, this training is held in the Mentoring Mansion and is done in an actual home environment.

After a year of successfully training women, Devi invited me to bring men in and equip them with marriage and home skills. I took her up on the offer and for two years I trained men in the practical aspects of their headship duties.

We had no idea the program would be such a success. Now, Mentoring Mansions are being planned for several cities in the nation.

We offered twelve classes to the men at the Mentoring Mansion. One of these classes taught "Manners and Etiquette." I was fairly certain this would not be the favorite class of the twelve presented. What *real* men would ever want to be groomed in manners, etiquette, and courtesy? I cringed thinking about it. I thought of asking John Wayne to please remove his hat at the table. I convinced myself that this one might not fly.

I couldn't have been more wrong. Men were curious and then actually eager to learn good manners. Some of the guys said it was their favorite session. I was shocked but happily so. One young man said, "Until now I've never felt comfortable taking a date out to a nice restaurant. Now I do." Like Gary, no one had taught this young man the skills he needed to act confidently at a nice table, and he was glad for the boost of self-confidence it gave him.

Several years ago the term *genteel* was used to describe a man that had polish and style. Though the word is rarely used these days, there's still an emphatic need for refinement in the male gender. The definition of genteel is "refined in manner—well-bred and polite—free from vulgarity or rudeness—elegantly stylish."

In traveling the world, I've noticed several places where men don't wear anything. And the only tie they wear is the one that sounds like the "B" string. In fact, on one of the islands that I visit regularly, Tanna Island, in Vanuatu, every other village is what they call a "cultural" village, meaning the only suit they wear is their birthday suits. I can handle that as long as I know they no longer eat missionaries.

However, in most places in the world, a modicum of modesty is still practiced, even though it changes according to the culture of the country. There is a code of etiquette and accepted behavior.

In America and other western cultures, casual style is now the mode—and manners, etiquette, politeness, chivalry, courtesy, courtliness, gallantry, and good grooming all went out with the Dark Ages—or at least many men think so. We have become such a generation of rude, crude, uncultured, uncouth, bad-mannered, foul-mouthed, coarse, and impolite men! To suggest that a man might want to consider becoming a gentleman sounds like an anachronism, something misplaced in time.

Men wear T-shirts shirts out in public imprinted with messages that are absolutely filthy. I'm embarrassed for the women minding their own business that might have the bad luck of coming up behind them only to be visually and verbally assaulted by the words and images on some of today's most popular "casual wear." Of course, some women wear similarly suggestive or vulgar clothes, but we'll leave them to my wife, Devi, to rebuke.

Where are the gentlemen of this world?

Where are the gentlemen of this world? Where are the men who treat their women like queens and their daughters like princesses? Where are the men who devote themselves to honoring and respecting their wives and their mothers? Where are the men who are schooled in courtesy and proper etiquette? Where are the gentlemen who know how to remove their caps for prayer and press their hands to their hearts when the flag passes by or the "Star Spangled Banner" is sung or played? Come on, guys, these habits and traditions are important and shouldn't be thought of as old-fashioned or pointless! In fact, you'll be admired—and, more importantly, provide a positive, role-model example to others—if you can display manners with a sincere attitude and presence of mind. You should never deploy these small etiquettes and manners as though annoyed. Attitude is as important as the action!

If we take the fatalistic approach that says, "Well, who am I to try and change the culture?" we will have failed our future generations of sons and young men. I, for one, am unwilling to turn a blind eye and pretend that crude and rude behavior doesn't matter. I will continue to pull out the chair for my wife, open her car door, escort her down the aisle, assist her with her coat, and give her my arm to lean on as long as I live. I even envision getting to heaven and asking Peter to please step aside, so I can open the door for my wife when she enters the pearly gates. To me, it still means something to be a gentleman. Furthermore, I still plan on drilling this into my sons-in-the-Lord!

I dread the day when men no longer wear ties, pull out chairs for ladies, or offer women their seats on a bus. I am dismayed to think that I might see the day when men no longer dress respectfully for church, wear suits to funerals and weddings, respond to people with, "Yes, sir" or "No, sir," or use proper etiquette when dining out. Dire will be the day when the uncouth "grunt" generation is all that is left.

It is so important that you teach your children proper etiquette! Training in good manners is a major building block in their childhood development. Actually, it is the foundation for teaching them respect, and respect is the bedrock of all discipline. Children, like trees, will grow crooked and warped without training and shaping. Training is like putting stakes and guide wires around trees so that they grow straight. The Bible doesn't say to *teach* a child in the way he should go, but *train* him. Training is more than just teaching or telling them. Training is showing them by example.

The Foundation of Etiquette

The foundation of all etiquette is kindness, which expresses itself by consideration for the people around you. Knowing proper etiquette makes you feel comfortable and assured enough to reach out to others and make them feel valued. Listen, if you're awkward and worried about how you should conduct yourself, you won't be able to focus on those others around you. Right? Believe me, the effort in learning manners pays great dividends.

What the Word Says

"Walk in a manner worthy of the calling with which you have been called, with all humility and gentleness, with patience, showing tolerance for one another in love" (Eph. 4:1-2, NASB).

Six hundred years before Christ, there were four princely, handsome, talented, and intelligent young Israelite men taken prisoner of war in Jerusalem and forced to march to Babylon. While there, Daniel and the three other Hebrew young men were required to serve in the king's palace. They were given a special diet (some of which they couldn't eat because it had been offered to idols), trained in ways of the Babylonian court, and taught the language of the Chaldeans.

The Bible says that at the end of the three-year training period they were ten times more skilled and learned than their Babylonian counterparts, and it was all because God had given them superior skills (Dan. 1:17-20).

I believe God wants his men to be superior in every way. We should know the meaning of grooming. We should be equally at home in the king's palace or eating on the floor of a humble hut in a remote village. We should be as comfortable dining at the table of royalty as we are enjoying an outdoor picnic with friends and family. The purpose of etiquette is so that we can be considerate and comfortable and confident in any social setting.

Casual is great. Baseball caps, sneakers, and jeans couldn't be better. But the truth is that in some settings they don't fit. "Casual" in a formal setting translates into sloppiness, ignorance, or insensitivity. The Fresh Prince of Bel Air might not object to your wearing sneakers to dinner, but the Crown Prince of Wales might.

If you are satisfied to reach and relate to only one strata of society, you can skip the rest of this chapter. But if you're interested in being "all things to all people so that you might reach some," then keep reading. I'll say it again: you can enhance your life, your influence, your impact in the world for God's kingdom by learning etiquette and manners.

Devi and I ministered for years to the hippies in the sixties and seventies. We loved welcoming teens into our church regardless of how they dressed. Many arrived wearing sandals, hot pants, and jeans and shirts "decorated" with stains, rips, and holes. Occasionally, we saw young men with no shirts at all! They were welcome to sit shirtless on our sofa leaving sweat and grime when they got up. Jesus loved them regardless of what they did or didn't wear, and so did we.

Dress never determined the depth or sincerity of our worship. However, we knew that if we didn't impart some cultural values we would be restricting the future impact of our young people. Now, if the only people they would ever reach were other hippies, then no problem. We wouldn't work on additional cultural and etiquette training. But most of the youth wanted to expand their opportunities for preaching the gospel. Occasionally, we'd run into a stubborn streak of independence or outright rebellion; still, most of our "kids" wanted to be trained. They were smart enough to keep their options open.

In all the years since then, we have been training youth and adults in the art of refinement. We couldn't have imagined there would be such a need within the body of Christ. But there is. We train, and then we watch our beloved students shine like new pennies. We're proud, and we know we've left something practical and transformational in our wake. There are no greater rewards in this life than to see you've helped or added to lives. We praise God he's placed us where we can do just that. He can use you to make a positive difference in your circles of influence as well. As a Teleios Man, your completion in Christ can contribute to his work of completion in others.

The list of courtesies and etiquette that I'm going to include below isn't exhaustive. It's a small set of guidelines and not the many hundreds of pages Emily Post would want you to read. It *will* provide a modest sense of decorum and establish some basics for a person who wants to be an example of gentlemanly behavior. You might want to put a check mark beside the bullet that describes something you want to add to your social graces. Think of this as finding and then using one more tool in your life as a Teleios Man.

Common Courtesies
(which have become much too uncommon)

- Open the door for both men and women when you arrive at the door first.
- Walk slightly behind a lady, then step forward to open the door. Remember, you are escorting and then presenting her. Don't walk ahead of your wife, unless you are going downstairs. When entering a room, walk behind her.
- Always open car doors for women.
- Remember to excuse yourself when walking in front of others.
- Pull out the chair for your wife or lady friend whenever you are seated in a restaurant. Seat her on your right.
- If a lady approaches your table in a public place, it is always appropriate to stand. If a man approaches your table, extend your hand with a cordial greeting.
- When shaking someone's hand, offer a firm handshake. The weak handshake is always remembered and can send an unintentional message of indifference.
- Assist senior citizens or handicapped people whenever possible.
- When people are talking to you, don't continue to watch television or continue to read. Pay attention to them.
- Assist women in putting on their coats.
- Walk guests to the door when they are leaving your home. If it is a lady without an escort, volunteer to walk her to her car, especially at night.
- When conversing with people, always look directly into their eyes. Eye contact is underrated.

- If all seats are taken and a woman is in need of one, volunteer yours. On a bus, train, or subway, if many people are standing it is not necessary.
- Don't read books or newspapers or use a cell phone when dining with others. Turn off that cell when a call will interrupt or annoy!
- Guys, you know this, but I'll cover the bases. Belching and other digestive noises are rude, uncouth, and have no place in a public context. It's not funny.
- When you are a guest at another's home, don't stay too long.
- Don't monopolize conversations. Learn when to stop talking and allow others to contribute to the conversation.
- When calling someone on the phone, introduce yourself as soon as they answer. "Hello, this is Larry Titus." When answering a phone, identify yourself first. "Hi, this is Larry Titus speaking."
- If you are a guest, take a gift with you for the hostess.
- When writing thank you notes, Christmas cards, or birthday cards, write in your own words and sentiments. The card's printed verse and your signature are not enough.
- Offer guests in your home something to drink. If you don't have anything else, offer water and ice.
- If you are an overnight guest in someone's home, return your toiletries to your room or suitcase rather than leaving them on the bathroom counter. After using the bathroom, use your towel to wipe off the sink and the tub.
- When guests are leaving your home, don't turn the lights off until they have departed.

Proper Table Conduct for the Guest

There are rules for every stage of a guest's dinner experience. You can learn the proper way to conduct yourself—from the time you are seated until the time that you leave the table.

Wait On the Hostess

- Wait for the host or hostess to assign you a place to be seated.
- After being seated at the table, wait for the hostess to be seated and then follow her leads.
- When the hostess puts her napkin on her lap, you follow. If she doesn't put her napkin on her lap but begins serving, then quietly place your napkin and continue.
- Never rearrange the table setting—even if it is set incorrectly. Remember that kindness does not embarrass the hostess who did not properly set her table. Instead, we choose to bend the rules and honor the hostess.

Passing the Food

- When dinner is being served continental style (the plate served in the kitchen and brought to the table), someone will set your plate in front of you, serving from the left. After eating, it will be removed from the right.
- If the food is served family style, you pass it to your right. However, do not lift a food dish to begin serving until the host or hostess begins passing the food.
- When serving family style, hold the dish for the person on your right while they serve their plate. They should then hold it for the next person and so on until it returns to you.
- To prevent accidents, avoid placing dishes on table's edge.
- When butter is passed, cut a piece of it using the butter knife. If one is not set, use your clean dinner knife. Put the butter on the edge of your bread plate (if none is set, use dinner plate); never serve the butter directly to your bread from the butter plate.
- Salt and pepper should be passed together at all times—even if someone says, "Please pass the salt." Always pick them up and pass them as a pair. The same is true with cream and sugar.

- When using sugar from a sugar bowl, do not use the sugar spoon to stir your beverage. Stir with another spoon, straw, or utensil.

During the Meal

- If a water or beverage glass is garnished with lemon or other decorative fruit, place the garnish in the glass before drinking. The garnish is for enhancing the flavor of the beverage, not for poking you in the eye or swiping your nose.
- When eating bread, break off a bite at a time, butter it, and eat it. Never butter the entire slice at once. This rule also applies to eating rolls and using jam or other spreads.
- Always use your knife to cut. Do not attempt to cut food with the side of your fork.
- Never place a soiled piece of silverware back on the table. Rest it on your plate. If the plate has been removed, rest the soiled silverware on an unsoiled piece of silverware.
- Eat with your mouth closed and do not talk with your mouth full. *Basic stuff, eh? But you wouldn't believe how many people ignore this one!*
- If you bite into a foreign object, simply remove it with your fingers and place it on your plate without saying a word. Do not spit it onto your fork or into your spoon.
- If you are served something that you do not care for, do not remove it, but leave it on your plate and eat around it.
- Under no circumstance should you ask for an item that is not served to the table. If the hostess discovers that she has forgotten something, she will let you know.
- If you must leave the table, ask to be excused. You need not give a reason for your departure. Return as quickly as possible.

- A centerpiece should not obstruct the view across the table. If it does, do not move it. Converse with the people who are beside you.

After the Meal

- When you have finished eating, place your soiled silverware on your plate. Even if some food remains on your plate, lay the utensils together on your plate. The handles of the silverware should not hang over the edge of the plate.
- Place your napkin unfolded at the left side of your plate.
- Thank your hostess for a wonderful time at her table. Compliment her for one item that she served. You might say, "Everything was delicious. I especially loved your dessert."

Years ago I received a booklet entitled *The Harness of Discipline.* It may still be in print, but it's been lost to my files for at least thirty-five years.

Recently, someone handed me an envelope at a Friday evening banquet, but I didn't open it until the weekend. It just so happened that minutes before I was to preach using a sermon I'd named "The Harness of Discipline" I opened the envelope to find a copy of the booklet. It was the same exact title as my message. Unless Alzheimer's has set in, I think I can dredge up from memory the gist of its message. If you have read this fable before, hopefully my version will at least resemble the original. If not, I claim editorial privileges.

The Harness of Discipline is a parable about a king's carriage that was driving down a road near an open pasture. Two wild stallions were there grazing.

The charioteer dismounted from his seat and engaged the two horses in conversation. "Would you be interested in becoming a part of the King's horses?" he asked.

"What would be required of us?" asked the horses.

"Why, you would have to be brought into the royal stables. Every morning you'd be awakened early. You'd be broken and trained, fed only the proper diet, and be disciplined many months and years in the ways of the royal horses. For only the best, most disciplined horses are allowed to pull the King's chariot. You must be willing to embrace the harness of discipline."

OK, I'll drop the C.S. Lewis style and head straight for the modern vernacular:

"I don't think so," said one of the horses. "Why would I want to leave my life of leisure and put on the harness of discipline? You've got to be crazy. Look, I can get up any time I want, go to bed any time I want, eat any time I want, and watch television any time I want." (OK, maybe the TV part wasn't in the original…)

Now let's also assume my horse using the modern vernacular is from Boston. He finished the conversation with the charioteer by saying, "Get outta heah!"

However, the other horse took the charioteer up on his offer and headed straight for the royal stables to begin his life of discipline.

Several years went by, and the King's chariot again went down this same road near the open pasture. This time the horse that had chosen the life of discipline was one of the horses in the royal team. As they approached the same field, the charioteer pulled up to speak to the remaining horse. This time, however, the green grass was dried up, the water ponds were empty, and the horse was gaunt and shabby.

The chariot came to a stop beside the open field. The lone stallion called with a plea from across the field. "Can I join the King's horses now? I'd love to pull the King's chariot."

"No," came back the stern reply. "If you're unwilling to submit to the King's discipline, you're unqualified to pull the King's chariot."

There is a discipline that the King of Kings demands. That's why he calls his followers "disciples." If you want a position in the elite team that pulls the chariot of a King, you must be groomed and disciplined. Likewise, if you want to be effective in Jesus's kingdom, it will require discipline, stewardship, and grooming.

Second Timothy 2:20-21 puts it this way: "In a large house there are articles not only of gold and silver, but also of wood and clay; some are for noble purposes and some for ignoble. If a man cleanses himself from the latter, he will be an instrument for noble purposes, made holy, useful to the Master and prepared to do any good work."

Culture, grooming, discipline, and etiquette are important in preparing us for the King's service. If we are willing to be trained in this school, we open doors to grand possibilities.

The hippies have come and gone. The refined lady and gentleman are still very much in demand. I don't think God or anyone else is interested in stuffy formality, but I do think a sense of deportment, decorum, and proper etiquette is always in fashion, even on the floor of a mud hut.

God wants to groom you for greatness. Are you willing to be coached and groomed? These small social graces we learn and then display speak eloquently of our commitments and our earnestness. Usually, they speak more loudly than words.

So, put your napkin in your lap, sit up straight, and pass to your right. Dinner is served.

Chapter 12

Your Legacy

REVEREND JOE BELIEVER

I OFTEN TRAVELED WITH MY parents on their evangelistic crusades. This was during the summer months, when I was in my late teens and early twenties. Mom was the best preacher of the two, but Dad did an incredible job of winning souls. They made a dynamic duo. Dad would lead people to the Lord during the day, and Mom would preach to them at night. When I traveled with them, I would play the piano or organ at the church services, and, since Dad was getting older, I would assist him with driving and handling the luggage.

One evening in Blackwell, Oklahoma, a man approached me at the organ as I played near the end of the service. He told me I had a telephone call waiting in the church office. When I answered the phone, I heard the voice of a friend who was the Superintendent of a denomination in the Northwest.

"Larry, I have recommended you to be the new District Youth President for Washington and Northern Idaho. Would you consider accepting the position?"

As I was telling him that I would "pray about it and get back to him," my mind was racing. *I've never preached before. I've never witnessed to people before. I don't consider myself "called" into the ministry. I don't even know why he would consider me for this position. He probably assumed that since I was a member of a ministry family that I had the needed experience.*

On my way back to the organ, I made a mental contract with the Lord. *Lord, they want me in Tacoma, Washington, by next Monday evening and this is already Wednesday evening. I don't have the money to take a bus, train, plane, or even drive to Washington. Plus, I've never done this before.* I continued my silent prayer, *If you will bring someone to me tonight who offers a ride to Washington State by Monday, I'll consider it a confirmation you're anointing me to preach your Word.* Having put my fleece before the Lord, I returned to the organ and continued playing for the altar service.

Within minutes, a couple approached me at the organ. "We wanted you to know, Larry, what a blessing your music has been to us. We wish we could stay longer, but we live in Seattle, Washington, and must leave tomorrow for home. Would you like to ride with us?"

I was speechless. I was stunned. I couldn't believe that God would answer my prayer so quickly and dramatically.

As soon as the service was over I returned the call to the superintendent. I told him I would accept the position and would speak at their youth rally on the following Monday evening.

I'd received astounding confirmation from the Lord. I was called into ministry that night. It's been forty-four years since I put my hand to the plow of ministry, and I haven't looked back! God started the process of making me one of his Teleios Men that day, and I've never had reason to question the trust I placed in him.

God called me in a very particular way that night. Did you know he's also called you? The New Testament pattern clearly demonstrates *everyone* is called into ministry. If you are born again, you're qualified to preach the gospel. You can be completed and perfected and matured in him. Believe it!

Jesus's "Great Commission," found in Matthew 28:19, sends us to make disciples of all nations and then teach these new disciples to obey everything he commanded. Jesus was sending all of us, not just professional clergy.

Scripture *does* identify the offices of pastor, apostle, prophet, teacher, and evangelist as gifts to the body of Christ for the *equipping of the saints*. In no way does the New Testament exclude believers from these functions. And he does not reserve the acts of witnessing, testifying, or otherwise sharing the gospel to any particular type of believer or type of giftedness.

Indeed, the responsibility for the ministry of the gospel belongs to all of us. Everyone is called!

In fact, you were ordained into ministry as soon as you were born again. John 15:16 is clear: "Ye have not chosen me, but I have chosen you, and ordained you, that ye should go and bring forth fruit, and that your fruit should remain: that whatsoever ye shall ask of the Father in my name, he may give it you" (KJV).

You Are an Ordained Minister

Ordination has come to mean the process whereby a person is vested into the office of minister, priest, or rabbi. The word has a very different meaning in Scripture. The biblical definition is far more inclusive. You see, every believer has been ordained by God to be fruitful in his kingdom. This means that whatever your gifts may be, they are to be used in reaching unsaved people with the gospel as well as blessing those already in the church. It's really that simple and foundational.

I'm not saying we don't need established and recognized "ordained" ministers in the church. But, I'll say it again: every believer has been ordained by God to be fruitful in his kingdom.

The word *ordained* in the Greek is *tithemi*. It means "to set, put, place, or lay an object down in a prone position." When the word is used relating to God's activity, it can mean past, present, or future action. For example, in Genesis 1:17, God sets (ordains) the stars in the firmament and in Psalm 8:3-4: "When I consider your heavens, the work of your fingers, the moon and the stars, which you have set (ordained) in place, what is man that you are mindful of him, the son of man that you care for him?"

In the New Testament, Mark 4:21 describes a light "set" on a lamp stand. Remember that the words *set* and *ordained* have the same meaning. John 15:16 is telling us Jesus intentionally *set* you in a certain position. He intentionally placed you in such a way that you will be effective and fruitful. God wants you to use your gifts to glorify him and spread his gospel. He wants you to recognize he's

All believers are part of God's royal priesthood and are ministers of the new covenant.

set you in a strategic position. Your pulpit could be in the marketplace. Your greatest anointing could come when ministering to your co-workers or your business associates in the daily grind of your profession.

All believers are part of God's royal priesthood and are ministers of the new covenant. So, it's ironic that Christians believe ministry should only be done by "professionals." This is completely contrary to the Word! It could even explain why revival lags in America but is vibrant in emerging countries. When new believers in those nations receive Jesus, they immediately start preaching the gospel. They don't have Bible College or Seminary training–they just go for it. Some of these new believers don't even have a complete Bible! They just know that they've been transformed. God is real, his Word is true, and his Spirit is powerful. Off they go on a lifelong trek to convert their people and introduce Jesus into their culture.

In America, when a person is born again, some mistakenly get the impression that his responsibility is to simply start attending church, become a faithful spectator, and help pay the preacher (the "professional") to fulfill the Great Commission.

Joe Believer is a "watcher" and has absolved himself—or so he thinks—of his responsibility to minister to the world. Scripturally, there is no such absolution, and there is no distinction between the sacred and the secular or the laity and the clergy. In Jesus, we are all one and everyone has a responsibility to fulfill the Great Commission.

You can be a businessman and be called into ministry without ever leaving your profession. Several years ago, I had the joy of performing the marriage ceremony for an amazingly gifted and beautiful couple who had been born again while attending a church service conducted at a business convention.

You can be a factory worker and minister to those on the assembly line. You can be a musician and rightfully consider yourself a minister of the gospel. You can be a school teacher and work to reach your students for Jesus. You can be an athlete and a minister of the gospel to your teammates, coaches, and fans. Wherever you are and whatever you do, God has commissioned you to be a minister of the gospel.

Preachers without Pulpits

Let me introduce you to a few ministers of the gospel we have come to know and appreciate over the years. Their lives exemplify Jesus's admonition to "make disciples of all nations."

Devi and I have close married friends who are both public school teachers. Each year, they pray they will be able to lead their students to Christ before that school year ends. I know of several coaches who openly witness about the reality of Jesus Christ to their athletes. A friend of mine owns a company with several hundred employees, and he regularly ministers Jesus to them. In fact, he has hired a full-time lay chaplain who ministers to them and counsels them on a daily basis.

Scores of my friends give abundantly to global missions. They think of missions as part of their regular budget. Many of the men I know who earn their living in construction make annual trips to foreign countries to work on churches, schools, orphanages, and medical facilities. One businessman I know has a full-time prayer intercessor who works on his staff. A man who owns a fleet of trucks prints scriptures to mount on the dashboards of the eighteen-wheelers. He gives the drivers worship music and sermon recordings to play during their drives. I know several men in law enforcement who are powerfully anointed to minister to people. Not a day goes by when they aren't preaching the gospel effectively to hurting people

We have a friend, Dr. Jack Herd, a chiropractor in Pennsylvania, who has a powerful anointing to minister healing to people. I don't know how many hundreds of people he has led to the Lord, or how many have been healed as a result of his ministry. One day, while he was doing an adjustment on a patient, a hair replacement specialist, he led the man to the Lord. Later, the hair specialist was sharing with one of his clients how he had been changed through his encounter with this chiropractor who told him about Jesus.

Though very religious, the hair specialist's client had a deep vacuum in his heart that religion couldn't satisfy. The testimony about a vital, living relationship with Jesus was all he needed to be born again.

Some time later, the hair specialist's son desperately needed ministry. He shared this with the newly born-again client. The hair specialist's client had begun attending a local church. He told the son about his new pastor. He was sure the pastor would happily minister to the hair specialist's son. Yep, this new pastor was me! I went immediately to the son who was transformed by the power of God.

As a result of the chiropractor's witness, the hair specialist, his client, and the hair specialist's son all found salvation in Christ and were entrusted to our ministry. But, here's the exciting thing. *I was the last one to do any ministering.* Everything took place in the daily warp and woof of the marketplace. The "clergy" weren't even involved.

Nothing excites me more than seeing people saved, healed, and delivered during the work week! Why? Well, they aren't responding to my preaching or a dynamic emotional altar call given on a Sunday. They've received ministry or were introduced to Jesus by an able minister of the gospel out in the marketplace.

I've met men from every type of profession and occupation who are doing an awesome job preaching the gospel in the so-called "secular" environment. What if every church member accepted his responsibility to spread the gospel? His obligation *is* as great as the pastor's obligation. What a difference it would make in the church if every man were to realize he was called to evangelize.

What if every Christian recognized we are all members of the body of Christ and every member is responsible for global evangelism? What if every believer understood we all are ministers of the gospel and responsible for finishing the work of ushering in the kingdom of God?

By simply assuming responsibility, more than half the battle in activating your calling is won. It doesn't mean everyone will become a pastor or an evangelist, but it certainly does mean everyone understands they are commissioned by Jesus to minister and evangelize. After all, the original world-changers, the disciples, had no formal training whatsoever. They just walked with the Master, and that qualified them to turn the world upside down.

I think most clergymen would be delighted to see all their congregants directly involved in reaching the world for Christ. When every member of the body is working, it makes the pastor's job much easier. The added blessing of every member working in the harvest field during the week is that when they arrive on Sunday to hear the sermon they're hungry rather than already "fed up." They're easy to feed when they've been working hard for the kingdom through the week, but woe to the pastor with a church full of people who have not been working for the Lord. There is no hunger for the Word of God and nothing satisfies them.

Release Your Calling

I would like to recommend that, from this moment, you consider yourself called and commissioned by Jesus Christ to preach the good news of the gospel to your family members, your friends, your neighbors, those you work with and, yes, the nations of the world as well. I also recommend you begin immediately preparing yourself for your calling. For some, it may well mean attending Seminary or Bible College, or going online for higher education in Bible training. God might want you to be part of that dedicated army of full-time ministers of the gospel who pastor local churches or evangelize at home or globally.

God has graced the body of Christ in this generation with an incredible array of godly, talented, principled men and women to lead his church and to fill the offices of apostle, prophet, pastor, evangelist, and teacher. Most of you, however, will find your place of ministry to be in the marketplace, and your training will involve the self-discipline of Bible study, prayer, fasting, generosity, and hospitality. Your ministry to the un-churched world makes you no less an anointed minister of the gospel than the full-time servants of the Word who minister weekly in pulpits. You might not be a "professional" minister, but you can be a professional who ministers. A life lived that way is on the Teleios Path.

Oliver Wendell Holmes said, "Alas for those that never sing, but die with all their music in them." I think the majority of American Christians go to their graves with the sermon still in them. God has set on you an anointing which qualifies you to reach the world. Whether you are seminary-trained or trained in the University of Hard Knocks, God has his hand on your life and has created you with unique ministry gifts. Consider yourself ordained!

Preparing for Ministry

If you want God to use you to preach his gospel in the world, you must begin by applying yourself to these principles:

Understand the priority of the kingdom of God in your life. (See Matthew 6:33). God's kingdom principles rule in every area of your life, including your time management, money, work, marriage and family, and other interests. Everything you do should be aligned with the goal of seeking first the kingdom of God. And please understand the kingdom of God is established when we take the gospel from inside the four walls of a church building to a hurting world outside. God's kingdom is extended through your ministry when people in the world are saved from sin through the blood of Jesus, set free from the oppression of Satan, and delivered from the kingdom of darkness into the kingdom of God. Be "kingdom" minded!

Study the Word as a lifestyle. Make it a part of your daily discipleship program. It's not only seminarians who need to study God's Word. It is an absolute priority for every believer. Study the Word, memorize the Word, feed on the Word, meditate on the Word, and preach the Word. Cultivate an intense love for the Word of God. Jesus quoted Deuteronomy 8:3b to the devil when he said, "Man does not live on bread alone, but on every word that comes from the mouth of the LORD."

Unless we know the Word of God, we will do little damage to the domain of darkness.

Practice serving people. The essence of ministry is found in serving. Although he was an apostle, Paul considered himself only a servant. Do you want to be in ministry? Start serving and you will be. God's priority is always people. This should always be our priority. A true servant never promotes himself or looks to his own interests. He looks to the interests of others.

Learn how to pray for others. The biblical word is *intercession*. Jesus is an intercessor (Rom. 8:34). The Holy Spirit is an intercessor (Rom. 8:26). God wants to make you, like Abraham, Moses, and Paul, an intercessor. An intercessor is one who "stands in the gap" for others. Intercession is the most selfless of all prayers because the object of the petition is other people. Any time you pray for others, you are interceding.

Love people lavishly. There is no ministry to people unless you love them deeply. The old saying is true, "People do not care how much you know until they know how much you care." 1 John 4:12 tells us, "No one has ever seen God; but if we love one another, God lives in us and his love is perfected in us." Do you want people to see God? Since God is invisible to mortal man, the only way people will ever see him is to see his love in you. Of all the sermons you ever preach, none will ever be greater than the love sermon you preach daily by the example of your own life.

Ask the Holy Spirit to reveal to you the needs of people around you. Humankind is hurting. Most people mask their needs out of pride and embarrassment. God the Holy Spirit knows where they hurt. He wants to reveal it to you so you can effectively minister healing to them. Unless you speak to their needs, you cannot bring deliverance to them.

Embrace God's refining process. God will use you, but first you'll be refined through trials. According to Hebrews 12:5-11, if you are not disciplined, you're an illegitimate child and not a true son. God requires his true sons to embrace his discipline in order that they might receive all the benefits of being a true son. Illegitimate children have no such benefits. In James 1 and 1 Peter 1, we are reminded of the value of trials and are encouraged to embrace them with joy. Too often, believers resist the trials which will groom them for God's service.

God uses tools that cut deeply and alter you forever. He'll use all kinds of people, situations, and circumstances in your life to dissect you, test your patience, and grind you down. You can count on it! There's a lot of rasping, sawing, and sandpapering ahead. But, good news! It's all for the purpose of making you into a vessel he can trust with his glory. That is how Teleios Men are made.

Brothers, this is a great place for a word of caution: bitterness and a lack of forgiveness will always keep you from experiencing God's release and anointing in your life. Hebrews 12:15 says, "See to it that no one misses the grace of God and that no bitter root grows up to cause trouble and defile many." Harboring bitter and unforgiving attitudes blocks the Holy Spirit from working through us in pure ministry to other people. We must guard our hearts against these negative and destructive attitudes. We minister powerfully when we are vessels, clean and available for the Master's use. Take it from me, if you want God to use you, keep bitterness and offense out of your heart.

Take a mission trip. The world becomes smaller when your vision becomes larger. Nothing will increase your vision more than a visit to destitute lands and peoples found in the developing nations. As you experience firsthand the brutal poverty and need, you'll never be the same. Your hurt will burn and you'll want to take action.

Never, and I mean never, belittle or put down other people's ministries. Don't even think about making yourself look more spiritual or effective by criticizing others. God's church is big, and he uses many different ministries and tools to get his work done. A person who ministers differently than you is not necessarily any less anointed or effective. You can ill afford to be arrogant in the harvest field for we all answer to the Lord of the Harvest. If God has graced you with a pulpit ministry, do not stoop to criticism of other pastors or churches. Jesus, as the head of the church, is well able to deal with those who occupy his offices. The Holy Spirit spoke to me one day while I was criticizing someone: "Larry, there's not room for another judge up here."

Inventory the gifts and abilities God has given you. You have incredible abilities and talents which God wants to use. Have you identified them? If not, why not? You do no wrong if you recognize your gifts and talents. Paul says in Romans 11:13, "…I make much of my ministry…" Your gifts, like the rod of Moses, can do everything from herding sheep to parting seas when you wield them for God. Your calling will reflect your gifts. God will call you into an area where your unique gifts will be powerfully and magnificently employed. So, what do you hold in your hand? What are the talents and aptitudes God has given you? You know, guys, these talents shine like jewels in your personality. I so encourage you to discover and refine them. You will realize God has given all of us gifts needed to reach the world in all manner of ways. It's your responsibility to steward them and make them available to the Master.

Jesus used a little boy's lunch to feed a multitude. What are those talents and abilities God has given to you? Men, I pray that you always recognize and turn your gifts over to God.

Allow the Holy Spirit to release his gifts—his *charismata*—through you. Gifts and miracles of healing, words of wisdom, words of knowledge, faith, prophecy, speaking in spiritual languages, and discerning of spirits will flow through you as the Holy Spirit pours out God's love. The gifts of the Spirit, listed in 1 Corinthians 12 and 14, were given to empower us to reach a lost world. Armed with these supernatural gifts, the disciples turned the world upside down in a few decades following the ascension of Christ. We must always remember: these gifts, these charismata, belong to God. We are only the conduit through which they flow. I don't possess or own the gift of healing. Rather, God *releases* the gift of healing through me. And remember to give God 100% of the glory when someone is touched and released through your ministry.

Make prayer a lifestyle. Prayer needs to be considered in the greater context of the life of Christ and the early church. The disciples could not cast out demons, Jesus said, because they didn't pray (Mark 9:29). The modern church in America today is largely powerless for the same reason. In my own experience, I spent several powerless years in my witness because I didn't understand the necessity of prayer. (See Luke 3:21, 5:16, 6:12, 9:18 and 9:28, 11:1-13, 18:1-8, Mark 1:35, Acts 1:14, 2:42, 4:29-31, 10:4, 9; 12:5.)

> *The power of God comes through prayer and the authority of God comes through knowing His Word.*

When you pray, you become a partner with God. Remember, God will never do anything of significance in your life unless you pray. The power of God moving in and through you is a direct result of your prayer life. Here's something you can quote me on: "The power of God comes through prayer and the authority of God comes through knowing His Word." Do as Paul commands in 1 Thessalonians 5:17, "Pray continually." I'll quote the newly revised Larry Titus translation: "Pray in the shower; pray in your pickup truck; pray walking down the street; pray with your wife; pray with your kids; pray on your job; pray on your cell phone; and pray on the internet. Pray everywhere and all the time."

Disciple people. Teaching people what they should do without training them how to do it produces frustration. Discipleship not only *teaches* people, but *trains* them as well. Jesus spent three-and-a-half-years training just twelve men. Yet, those twelve men circled the globe with God's love.

Family members are our most important discipling prospects. Train them well in the special classroom of your home. Your family and your home are the foundation of the church.

Rick Warren, the Pastor of Saddleback Church in California and author of *The Purpose Driven Life*, was recently interviewed by Paul Bradshaw. Rick is an ultimately anointed man of God. His sage comments fit well in the context of this chapter. When asked the question, "What is the purpose of life?" Rick responded: "In a nutshell, life is preparation for eternity. We were made to last forever, and God wants us to be with him in Heaven."

Rick went on to say, "One day my heart is going to stop, and that will be the end of my body—but not the end of me. I may live sixty to one hundred years on earth, but I am going to spend trillions of years in eternity. This is the warm-up act—the dress rehearsal that God wants us to practice on earth what we will do forever in eternity. We were made by God and for God, and until you figure that out, life isn't going to make sense.

"Life is a series of problems: Either you are in one now, you're just coming out of one, or you're getting ready to go into another one. The reason for this is that God is more interested in your character than your comfort. God is more interested in making your life holy than he is in making your life happy. We can be reasonably happy here on earth, but that's not the goal of life. The goal is to grow in character, in Christ-likeness…

"You can focus on your purposes, or you can focus on your problems. If you focus on your problems, you're going into self-centeredness, which is, 'my problem, my issues, my pain.' But one of the easiest ways to get rid of pain is to get your focus off yourself and onto God and others…

"We need to ask ourselves: Am I going to live for possessions? Popularity? Am I going to be driven by pressures? Guilt? Bitterness? Materialism? Or am I going to be driven by God's purposes [for my life]?

"When I get up in the morning, I sit on the side of my bed and say, 'God, if I don't get anything else done today, I want to know You more and love You better.' God didn't put me on earth just to fulfill a to-do list. He's more interested in what I am than what I do. That's why we're called human beings, not human 'doings.'

"In the happy moments, PRAISE GOD. In the difficult moments, SEEK GOD. In the quiet moments, WORSHIP GOD. In the painful moments, TRUST GOD. And, in every moment, THANK GOD."[*]

Amen, Brother!

There are three things that flood my normally dry eyes with tears.

First, I cry easily when I'm exposed to anything patriotic. I love this country. I love those who serve in the armed forces, and I love the beautiful flag of the United States. July 4th ceremonies invariably play upon the deepest strings of my heart. Buglers playing taps at the gravesite of a veteran release a flood of emotions and gratitude in me.

Secondly, I cry whenever I see seasoned missionaries and wizened indigenous leaders who have sacrificed their lives for Christ to see their nations saved. May my tears wash their feet.

---

[*] Interview posted on CCNews Portal, August 12, 2006, http://www.ccnews.org/index.php?mod=Story&action=show&id=2449&countryid=207&stateid=0.

Thirdly, I cry when I see the Holy Spirit separating people into the ministry. I have often been called upon to lay hands on people in services of ordination. I hardly get the words, "Preach the Word, be instant in season and out of season," out of my mouth before a faucet opens and the tears flow.

But I'm equally as touched when I see God working through those of you who toil daily in the marketplace. Your anointing is no less powerful than those whom God calls to the five-fold offices in the church. Please understand how deeply covered you are with the Holy Spirit! Please know how powerfully God is going to use you in the world. Your potential to reach people with the gospel is far greater in the marketplace than you can imagine. But I have one fear; I fear that you will not understand that the anointing on you is as great as it is on anyone else. The tears I shed for you are tears of compassion, praying that you will awaken to the incredible anointing that God has on you to reach into the deepest corners of darkness.

Businessman, carpenter, electrician, banker, CEO, CFO, COO, CPA, school teacher, coach—you have been ordained by Jesus Christ to bring forth fruit and that your fruit should remain. Go and preach the gospel of Jesus Christ to all the world. The same Holy Spirit that anointed Jesus is the Holy Spirit who anoints you. And always, always know you have a spiritual dad named Larry Titus who prays and holds you before the Lord. I am so proud of you! May your works multiply and may you show Jesus to the world!

DISCIPLESHIP

Regardless of your skills, calling, anointing, passion, mission or profession, there is something that every man has been called to do and that is to disciple men. Jesus' final words to the disciples prior to his ascension make it crystal clear, "Go and make disciples of all nations...." Matthew 28:19. Dallas Willard calls this The Great Omission." It's the most important task of the church, but rarely is it seen as anything more than a surface level suggestion in most people's minds.

Are you kidding me? How better to trivialize the final words of Jesus and the summation of everything that he did by not doing it?

The church in general and men in particular have never understood that making disciples in the same way that Jesus did is critical for our growth, their growth and the only method of global evangelism. We have never understood that discipleship is not optional. Either we disciple men or we fail to fulfill the great commission and turn it into, as Willard says, the Great Omission.

I pray that in these final pages you will catch my heart, my burden, my passion to see men transformed into the image of Jesus precisely because of your investment in them.

I Love Men

This is the last chapter of a book I have written lovingly and with a great father's heart for men. I will nurture and protect and disciple men until I draw my last breath! I will be a surrogate father to those guys needing me, and I will continue to rescue, reclaim, and disciple men who are hurt, battered, and lost.

- *I love to see men released in their calling.*
- *I love to see men train their sons and daughters to love God.*
- *I love to see men raise holy hands in praise to God.*
- *I love to see men hug, kiss, and hold hands with their wives.*
- *I love to see men wrestle with their sons.*
- *I love to see men hug their kids.*
- *I love to see men talk about Jesus without embarrassment.*
- *I love to see men work hard to provide an income for their families.*
- *I love to see men reaching out to other men with the love of God.*
- *I love to see men taking vacations with their families.*
- *I love to see men who are not afraid to cry in public.*
- *I love to see men stand against sin.*

- *I love to see men take their daughters out on daddy-dates.*
- *I love to see men praying with other men.*
- *I love to see men treating women with respect, honor, and sensitivity.*
- *I love to see men assume leadership responsibilities in the home, church, and marketplace.*
- *I love to see men take responsibility for their home, family, and marriage.*
- *I love to see men who aren't afraid to hug another man in expressions of God-honoring affection.*
- *I love to see men who are willing to be spiritual fathers and mentors to other men.*

It's simply a fact: I love men. I mean I really love them! I love men the way Jesus loved men. He loved them, trained them, and released them to become what he was—a fisher of men. The disciples just fished for fish until they met Jesus. Little did they know their first encounter with Jesus on the shores of Galilee would do more than take them away forever from their nets. That encounter would soon change their lives, and the course of the world.

Men, please hear me; this is so important! Jesus wants the same from you! He wants to transform your life, and then he'll work through you and transform the lives of other men. He wants you deeply involved in a discipleship program where you are spiritually mentored and fathered by someone further along in the faith than you, so you in turn can become a father and mentor to other men.

What It Means to Be a Disciple

Jesus spent nearly every moment with the twelve men he chose to follow him. He taught them daily for three-and-a-half years using parables and real life illustrations. He taught them to pray. He showed them how to do the will of the Father. He revealed the meaning of scripture. He taught them in practical ways how to implement the kingdom message by praying for the sick, preaching the gospel of peace, ministering to the poor, and delivering those oppressed by Satan. Most of all, he *trained* them with the example of his life. Then, Jesus departed and left them with his final words found in Matthew 28:19-20. Essentially he told them, "You've seen me do it; now it's your turn."

For centuries, young boys were tutored by older craftsmen until they could perform the same tasks with identical dexterity and quality. Though rare today, this type of apprenticeship training is still found on the farm, in some labor unions, and in specific internships, such as the medical profession. Such training is patterned after Jesus's methods with the twelve men. We must find someone who is further along in the faith than us, latch on to their coattails, and follow them!

Paul's exhortation and invitation is simple and straightforward in 1 Corinthians 11:1, "Follow my example, as I follow the example of Christ." The Greek word for *follow* literally means to "mimic." To imitate or mimic a trustworthy spiritual guide as that person imitates or mimics Christ is a perfect description of discipleship. In other words, whatever the role model does in keeping with Christ's example, we can do it too. Pure discipleship is not a series of lectures on Christian subjects or doctrines set in a church environment. It is a lifestyle of training created and modeled by the teacher and followed by the student.

First, Be a Disciple

To be a leader, you must first learn to be a follower. The disciples could never have had the life of Christ in themselves without first following after him here on earth. Before you can live your own life with direction, wisdom, and discipline, you must first have seen these traits lived and modeled by others.

To be a leader, you must first learn to be a follower.

Don't listen to the pious who say something like, "Don't follow a man." This is flatly the worst advice you could hear. Who else can we follow? God is no longer walking around in the flesh. He left eleven men who were to take his authority and do exactly as he did—go into all the world and make disciples.

You must be willing to become a *disciple* so you can one day become a *disciple-maker.*

True discipleship never produces clones; it produces godly, healthy, mature men—Teleios Men!—with distinct personalities and gifts. Show me a man who has been tutored by another mature, qualified Christian man, and I'll show you a great leader. That's how they are made. Great leaders are not born. They are made by observing and imitating other great leaders. Following a man who is a true discipler and teacher will not make you a mindless clone. A man left to his own devices matures more slowly (if at all) and is much more vulnerable. He won't have the emotional intelligence, savvy, and people skills as will those trained by others.

Imagine a surgical resident telling senior physicians that he could do a better job on the patient if he could be left to discover for himself how to perform surgery.

We all need the well-intentioned input, experienced wisdom, and practical advice that trained, well-seasoned men offer. To believe otherwise is to remain untaught and underdeveloped as a kingdom servant. The Christian world must use Jesus's example and disciple men by the honing and training of truly qualified leaders.

We hear that men are "visual" and learn best through visual presentation. Every man needs a leader in his life who looks, acts, and talks like Jesus. Then he can eventually look, act, and talk like Jesus as well. I may be naïve, but I think deep down in the soul of every man is a heart cry to be discipled, coached, and shown the way by another man—a father figure, a mentor.

Fellowship is great and necessary, but we all need someone more seasoned in the faith with life experiences who will walk alongside us to disciple, guide, encourage, and affirm us. Men need examples—good ones. We need to be shown what it means to be a godly father, husband, leader, and man of God. We also need someone who can pull us out of harm's way—at least shout a warning—and get us back on track when we get off course. There's nothing like a stern but loving finger in the face that says, "Larry, don't do that! It will damage your future and mar your character!"

My own early discipleship opportunities were few and far between. There were not many men I could look to as spiritual fathers, examples, and mentors. Though I didn't know it at the time, even by my late teens I was looking for this type of mentor to be a part of my life. Someone did walk into my life, but after a few months, walked out again. But it was enough to keep me going in the right direction.

When I was seventeen, I went to one leader and asked if I could buy him lunch so I could talk with him. At the time, I knew no one else I respected as much as I did this godly, dynamic Christian leader. While we were talking, I awkwardly blurted out, "Do you mind if I follow you?" I don't remember his response exactly, but I do remember attempting to follow him. Wherever he was, I would try to get around him so I could see what he did and hear what he said. I wanted to imitate his life. I wanted to learn and be shown the ropes.

There have been a few other leaders I followed through the years, but most of them affected me from a distance. It was impersonal, and I took my cues more from observation than through hands-on training. As soon as I saw a leader who exhibited spiritual success and integrity, I sought to synchronize with him and replicate his life.

Sadly, there was no leader who brought me into his life. I desperately wanted to track alongside a godly man and watch him in action. I don't remember any hand on my shoulder or a voice that said, "Larry, I believe in you. I want to train you to be a great Christian and a great leader."

Since my dad died when I was fairly young, the greatest influence in my adult life was definitely my mother. She spoke volumes of wisdom into me, and I praise God daily for her investment. I can't help but wonder, though, what my leadership would be like today if there had been a man who believed in me enough to invest his leadership skill, wisdom, and loving correction in my life.

So, that's why I do what I'm doing today. I'm helping men answer questions—questions that went unanswered in my own life..

It is my heart's desire that men will have strong available leaders and mentorship. However, here's an immediate question for you, as a reader: *Do you have the heart of a disciple?* Are you a teachable man, a guy who is willing to follow in the footsteps of someone who is further along in the faith? Are you willing to slip into the "Harness of Discipleship" to fulfill the words of Jesus?

How to Succeed as a Disciple

Discipleship has one golden rule. Memorize this rule and repeat it to yourself: *A disciple must be both teachable and correctable.* You must have both characteristics. A teachable person will always grow, develop, and mature. A correctable person will remain non-defensive and will always be open to improvement. The defensive nature of a man is one of the greatest obstacles to discipleship. I remember the many times I would try to teach my son something only to hear, "I know, Dad, I know."

"No, you *don't* know, Son. That's why I'm trying to teach you." Be teachable!

Even now I still correct myself. I work at not having an attitude of "I know, I know…" I don't say it out loud, but it's not uncommon for me to respond to someone's suggestions with the same childish I-already-know-it-already attitude. As soon as I think or say "I know," I deflect a chance to learn something, and, all too often, I only thought I already understood the point I was dismissing as old news.

Write it down in your notes as a reminder. If you refuse to be corrected, you choose to stop changing, and you'll miss new or better ideas. Look at it this way: if you are open and willing to consider other people's ideas, you can add to what you already know. You can multiply your ideas, experiences, and information dozens or even hundreds of times. But if you refuse to consider another person's advice or suggestions, you're restricted to information you've already gleaned. Do you want to live in a small world or a large world? The choice is yours.

Good disciples turn into good leaders.

If you're open to the advice, counsel, and ideas of others, you will never stop growing. The knowledge of the world is yours for the listening and learning. But no one can feed someone who is already fed up. You can only feed those who are hungry. Get your antennae up and your ears turned to all the information you can get, especially from those you know to be disciple makers. This doesn't mean you're to be vulnerable or you should blindly accept every new philosophy that comes down the pike. It does mean your heart should remain teachable and correctable. Good disciples turn into good leaders. It's just that simple.

Where Are the Fathers?

Deep in the heart of every man is the desire for a dad. Many men have never had a real dad, let alone a spiritual father. Countless guys had biological fathers who rejected or abused them. I don't think there is any wound in a man that cuts deeper or causes more emotional scarring than the wound of not having a father. You might not see it or hear it, but men's hearts cry out for the strong unconditional love, embrace, and acceptance of a father.

You've heard the statistics about boys who grow up fatherless. While not every boy experiences the same pain and turmoil, I've yet to meet one who didn't yearn for a healthy, loving relationship with a dad. Obviously, the ultimate father experience comes when a man or boy meets Father God through a relationship with Jesus Christ. Yet, we still need, we crave consciously or otherwise, a relationship with an earthly counterpart who models the loving nature of God the Father.

Where are the fathers? We can paraphrase what the Apostle Paul said in 1 Corinthians 4:15: though we have ten thousand paid teachers, we don't have many fathers. I'll say a hearty "Amen!" to that. And I'll tell you after decades of experience all over the globe, ministering and watching, the ratio is just about that small. Truly, there are no more than a few fathers amongst the thousands of those who teach.

As I travel and speak at men's and pastors' conferences across the nation and throughout the world, I rarely find a man who is willing to become a spiritual father to men outside his immediate family. Yet, I find thousands of "sons" who thirst and yearn for fathers. Ten thousand paid teachers and pastors are everywhere, and they're willing to preach. Few are willing to spiritually sponsor another man. They simply push away from the great effort and sustained commitment required to train men.

It's easy to shake a man's hand following the sermon. It is another thing altogether to meet him one-on-one, face-to-face over coffee and help them *personally*. It's easier to keep them at arm's length and say, "Listen to me," than suggest, "Follow me." It's more comfortable to keep a safe distance between the pulpit and the pew than to let a man into our life on a regular basis. Such a ministry requires more transparency, vulnerability, and sacrifice than many paid workers are prepared to give.

The foregoing little sermon was, of course, for preachers—the "ten thousand" that Paul described. However, the scripture doesn't limit mentoring to pastors exclusively. Mentoring is a calling for every man. If you're further along in Christian maturity and godliness than another man, then make yourself available to take him under your wing and mentor him. Become a spiritual dad to a son. It's that easy, and it's also that hard. You'll be giving from your own life, but the rewards are spectacular and will live through future generations.

For years I've had a prison ministry. I was eighteen years old when I began sharing Jesus in California's San Quentin Prison. It didn't take me long to discover it was a lot easier to lead men to Christ than it was to disciple them. All I had to do was to tell them about Jesus, have them repent of their sins, hand them a Bible, and tell them to pray. The cell door slammed shut, and I was on my way. Discipleship, on the other hand, was an entirely different ball of wax. "You mean I have to teach him how to save money, to love his enemies, to treat his wife and kids with respect, and to obey the law?" Precisely! I had to do all that.

In one instance, I took a man who had been released from prison directly to a shopping mall so he could buy some civilian clothes. He came back twenty minutes later with a gold bracelet. He had conned a clerk at a jewelry kiosk into giving him the expensive bracelet on credit. "Take it back," I firmly insisted. "You can't have a gold bracelet until you earn the money to pay cash for it."

Yes, it's easier to get people saved than to get them on the discipleship track. Maybe that's why we have more preachers than mentors. It's easy to preach but difficult to disciple. Functioning as a father requires more strength and fortitude than does merely acting as an advisor. A father is down in the ditches and trenches, sweating and swinging pick and shovel. An advisor only points to where he thinks the digging should go.

Malachi prophesied in the last chapter of the Old Testament that God would send the prophet Elijah before the coming of the great and dreadful day of the Lord. Malachi prophesized that Elijah would turn the hearts of the fathers to the children and the hearts of the children to their fathers.

This verse sounds so simple. Yet, how profound it is! The last thing to occur before the return of the Messiah is for dads to become fathers again, and for alienated children to be restored to fathers.

Are we seeing fathers and children restored? More importantly, are we *doing* it? When we look out over the landscape and see the carnage resulting from broken or non-existent father and child relationships, we must be deeply moved and concerned. Our hearts must break, and we must begin the work of restoration. We must be in the ditches and trenches, working and sweating to dig our way back to our children. We must make a way for them to come back to us.

There are some flickers of hope and encouraging signs. Many new ministries to fathers have emerged and are continuing to emerge. Discipleship programs begin and abound, books appear on the shelves of Christian bookstores, and mega-events call for the return of fathers to their families. Do these efforts keep pace with increasing divorce rates, desertion of families by the fathers, and alienation of dads from their children through emotional and physical abuse? Only God knows.

My prayer is that God will reverse the curse of centuries of abdication by fathers and give the men of this nation a hunger to return to their children. My heart cries to see sons spiritually adopted by mature, godly men. I'll never rest or be satisfied until hundreds of thousands of suffering spiritual orphans are adopted and taken under the wings of able men. These able men are everywhere and walk the face of this earth. I again pray that such men hear the cries of the orphans.

I Looked for a Father

At a pastors' conference in South Carolina I was speaking of the need for men to be discipled by spiritual fathers. A pastor in the audience raised his hand and said, "I've looked for years for a man to be a spiritual mentor and father to me and can't find one. What do I do? I've even asked them personally if they would mentor me and they've refused." My answer was to keep praying and keep looking and to do so with single-mindedness and to never stop seeking such a leader.

In the meantime, *be to someone else what you've never had.* Be a spiritual father. How can you give what you've never received? Every parent knows that children come with their own operator's manual. Even if your own upbringing was not the best, something inside you instinctively knows what children need. We do our best, and God makes up the deficit. Here's a powerful secret: Our *intentions* are honored and empowered by God.

My own life proves that not having had a spiritual mentor doesn't preclude a person from being one. With the Word of God as our manual, and the love of God as the compelling force in our hearts, we can become that kind of man. This is the Teleios Principle in action. We all need spiritual dads, and we all need to *become* spiritual dads. There is no greater need in the world today than the need for fathers who love their children—both natural and spiritual—as God the Father loves his children.

How to Become a Spiritual Dad

Be the person who, first and foremost, offers the essential basic ingredient: love. You can't disciple a person you don't love. You're doing more than simply imparting information to a younger or less mature man; you're investing in him. You're seeking to bring out the best in him and to see him become everything God intends him to be. The teaching process alone is not enough. You must become his coach and trainer. The training process involves showing as well as teaching. To do that, you must allow him into your life. This is not a classroom lecture. This is a true life encounter whereby a person sees you as you are, with your faults and foibles. It's about your willingness to be totally transparent so he can see "all" of you.

Be a gold digger. In every man there is gold, and I'm determined to find it. There's also dross and sludge we have to be willing to dig through first. Always remember to focus on the gold in a person. We can praise God that Jesus didn't stop working on us as soon as he saw the garbage in our lives. His grace covers us while he brings out the gold. We need to offer others the same grace God has extended to us.

Let them into your life. I allow them to track after me and see how I do things. I teach them how to study the Word, how to pray, how to treat their wives and children, and how to edify others. I let them participate in my family activities. I remember their birthdays. I call them often. I meet them for dinner. I encourage them. I help them discover their qualities and gifts.

Take them along. I invite men on trips and to my home. I affirm them and let them know they're special. I pray for them and with them often.

Offer correction only in the context of empathetic love. The purpose of correction must always be redemptive. They must know how much I want them to succeed. Correction cannot come simply because I'm ticked-off or mad at them. I usually spend months and, in some cases even years, before I offer any form of correction. I reject the words *constructive criticism*. That's an oxymoron. In my mind, all forms of criticism are destructive, not constructive. Correction is an important element of change and growth, but criticism—merely pointing out a person's faults—tears down a man's spirit. If I recognize something in their lives so destructive it will keep them from succeeding, I will broach the subject only after a great deal of prayer, seeking God's wisdom to not only expose the problem but also to provide the answer.

Give men opportunities to use their gifts and talents in a safe environment. Remember, disciples must have opportunities to fail safely, not fearing they'll be criticized if things don't work out as planned. Failure is an essential part of success. If a person is not allowed to fail, he will never learn to succeed or enjoy the fruit of success.

Find God's fingerprints on them. I search to discover individual uniqueness and gifts in hopes of seeing indications of God's sovereign plan for their lives and futures. John the Baptist was able to identify the gifts and calling of Jesus. Every man has a God-ordained identity that needs to be confirmed by others.

Jesus said in John 5:31 that if he were to testify about himself, his testimony would be invalid. The same is true with everyone. You need someone in your life who will bear witness to your gifts and calling in Jesus. You need someone who can help you identify and release your anointing. Why not be the person who can speak prophetically into someone else's life? Why not be like John the Baptist to another believer?

I want you to read a letter from Ken. Ken is one of my more recently adopted sons from New England. He sent this letter after attending one of our Men's Summit in California:

> Dear Pastor Larry:
>
> Blessings to you, mighty soldier in God's Army. This is Ken from BAC. [BAC is a Christian rap group from New England.] First off, I wanted to thank you for the incredible weekend that we had in Irvine. I am blessed and honored to receive invitations to these life-changing events. My life was certainly changed. I think that weekend showed me some things that I've been forsaking for way too long. For the past couple years, I'd been so caught up in the business of ministry that I'd forgotten the absolute preciousness of intimacy with God and the preciousness of relationships with people of faith, specifically men.
>
> Hearing the testimonies of some of the brothers made my heart burst all over again. As I told you in Denny's, I realized just how much I have no clue of the depth and richness of God's grace. I thought I had somehow figured it out, and I think that's when some stagnation began to seep in to my life. I know now that God is so big, so incredible, so beyond my limitations, and new in my life every day. I will definitely be back next year (wherever it is) and have been keeping contact with some of my newfound brothers in the faith.
>
> Secondly, I realized that weekend why everyone calls you "Dad." Previously I knew it in my head, but now I know it in my heart. Honestly, I'd never had the desire (for lack of a better word) to call you

"Dad," but I couldn't figure out why. I grew up fatherless and have always longed for a dad; it's just that I accepted from a very young age that I would be fatherless for life, and that was it. When Christ found me and I accepted him and my New Father, God gave me so much that I was lacking and really taught me how to be a man. Still I didn't think I could actually have a dad or feel closeness with a "father." In Irvine, I realized the necessity of relationship, contact, and touch with other brothers in the faith, and that it's possible to make up the lack with an "adopted" dad.

Though I needed a dad so desperately, I still wasn't convinced I could call you "Dad" until the other night when I awoke from a dream. In the dream, you and I had met again after a long absence and embraced, much the same way I think a father and son would. I called you "Dad," and it felt twenty-five years right. So, if it's OK with you, I'd like to call you Dad.

Thirdly, I know you know, but I wanted to tell you that you have some incredible men around you. Brothers like Jeff and Ricky and Tyran are just amazing, and they ministered to me profoundly in Irvine. I've never met a man that has understood and practiced the Jesus/Disciple relationship like you do. Maybe more than anything, I took from Irvine the model of imparting things into special men and making them more special. Speaking into them virtue and blessing, helping to draw out the wonderful God-given gifts inside of them. You've done that magnificently, and the evidence is the men whom you've touched.

Thank you again for everything, I look forward to seeing you again soon.

Your son,

Ken

Ken received God's message of hope and his challenge to grow into a Teleios Man—"…to the measure of the stature which belongs to the fullness of Christ" (NASB). I'm happy for him and proud of him, and God gets the glory. That message and challenge goes out with love to each of us. That's God's perfect plan for completing the perfect man, one imperfect but teachable man at a time.

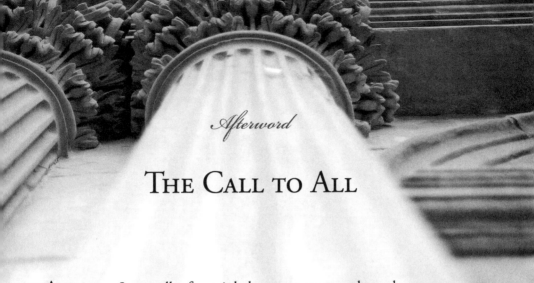

THE CALL TO ALL

A S FAR AS I can tell, after triple bypass surgery and two heart stents, I've got another fifty thousand miles or twenty years left on my life, whichever comes first. Oh yes, or unless Jesus returns before then. And between now and then I have committed myself to mentoring other men. I consider it the greatest calling of my life. I would like you to consider it your greatest calling as well.

There's a rich and awesome world of men out there who need just one man to put an arm on their shoulder and say, "You can do it!"

Would you consider helping me? If so, please go to our website and register as a man who is committed to being a spiritual mentor and father to another. I'm not trying to assign you disciple status. I merely want to hear from you that I've touched your heart and you're willing to make yourself available to be a spiritual dad to someone as one of the ways you participate in the fulfillment of the Great Commission. Our web site is www.teleiosman.com.

I look forward to spending eternity with you, along with a line of men in heaven as far as the eye can see who will say, "I'm here because of you."

> After that, we who are still alive and are left will be caught up together with them in the clouds to meet the Lord in the air. And so we will be with the Lord forever. (1 Thess. 4:17)

BIBLIOGRAPHY

Arterburn, Stephen and Fred Stoeker. *Every Man's Battle: Winning the War on Sexual Temptation One Victory at a Time*. Colorado Springs: WaterBrook Press, 2009.

Arterburn, Stephen and Fred Stoeker. *Every Man's Challenge: How Far Are We Willing to Go for God?* Colorado Springs: WaterBrook Press, 2004.

Bright, Bill.

Elliot, Jim. *Shadow of the Almighty*. London: Hodder and Stoughton, 1958.

Friel, John and Linda. *The 7 Worst Things Parents Do*. Deerfield Beach, FL: Health Communications, Inc., 1999.

Gallagher, Steve. *At the Altar of Sexual Idolatry*. Dry Ridge, KY: Pure Life Ministries, 2000.

George, Bob. *Classic Christianity: Life's Too Short to Miss the Real Thing*. Eugene, OR: Harvest House Publishers, 2010.

Giuliani, Rudolph. *Leadership*. New York: Miramax, 2005.

Hayford, Jack. *The Anatomy of Seduction*. Ventura, CA: Regal Books, 2004.

Hayford, Jack. *Fatal Attractions: Why Sex Sins Are Worse Than Others*. Ventura, CA: Gospel Light Publications, 2004.

Hayford, Jack. *Sex and the Single Soul: Guarding Your Heart and Mind in a World Full of Empty Promises*. Ventura, CA: Regal Books, 2005.

Morris, Robert. *The Blessed Life: The Simple Secret of Achieving Guaranteed Financial Results*. Ventura, CA: Regal Books, 2004.

Roberts, Ted. *Pure Desire*. Ventura, CA: Regal Books, 2008.

Warren, Rick. *The Purpose Drive Life*. Grand Rapids, MI: Zondervan Publishing Company, 2002.

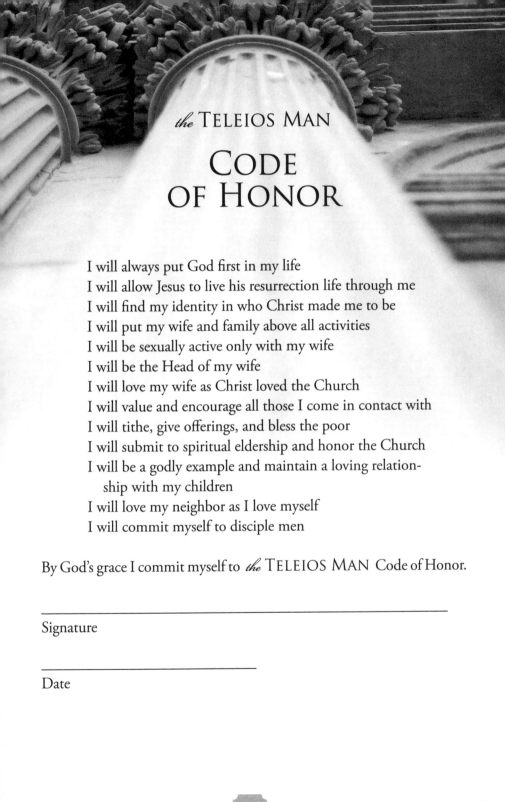

the TELEIOS MAN

CODE
OF HONOR

I will always put God first in my life
I will allow Jesus to live his resurrection life through me
I will find my identity in who Christ made me to be
I will put my wife and family above all activities
I will be sexually active only with my wife
I will be the Head of my wife
I will love my wife as Christ loved the Church
I will value and encourage all those I come in contact with
I will tithe, give offerings, and bless the poor
I will submit to spiritual eldership and honor the Church
I will be a godly example and maintain a loving relation-
   ship with my children
I will love my neighbor as I love myself
I will commit myself to disciple men

By God's grace I commit myself to *the* TELEIOS MAN Code of Honor.

_____

Signature

_____

Date

IF YOU'RE A FAN OF THIS BOOK, PLEASE TELL OTHERS…

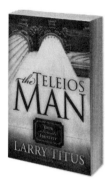

- Write about *The Teleios Man* on your blog, Twitter, MySpace, or Facebook page.
- Suggest *The Teleios Man* to friends.
- When you're in a bookstore, ask them if they carry the book. The book is available through all major distributors, so any bookstore that does not have *The Teleios Man* in stock can easily order it.
- Write a positive review of *The Teleios Man* on www.amazon.com.
- Send my publisher, HigherLife Publishing, suggestions on websites, conferences, and events you know of where this book could be offered.
- Purchase additional copies to give away as gifts.

CONNECT WITH ME…

To learn more about *The Teleios Man* and Kingdom Global Ministries, please visit www.kingdomglobal.com or contact my publisher directly:

HigherLife Development Services, Inc.
400 Fontana Circle
Building 1—Suite 105
Oviedo, Florida 32765
Phone: (407) 563-4806
Email: info@ahigherlife.com

OTHER RESOURCES TO SUPPORT YOUR HOME AND FAMILY RELATIONSHIPS

- *The Teleios Man* Workbook and DVD Set
- *The Table Experience*
- *The Home Experience*

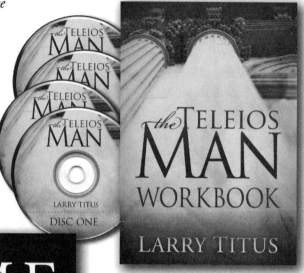

To order these resources go to www.kingdomglobal.com/store